Shopify Application Development

Build highly effective Shopify apps using the powerful
Ruby on Rails framework

Michael Larkin

BIRMINGHAM - MUMBAI

Shopify Application Development

First published: May 2014

Production Reference: 1210514

Published by Packt Publishing Ltd.
Livery Place
35 Livery Street
Birmingham B3 2PB, UK.

ISBN 978-1-78328-105-3

www.packtpub.com

Cover Image by Benoit Benedetti (benoit.benedetti@gmail.com)

Credits

Author
Michael Larkin

Reviewers
Joey deVilla
Christophe Favresse
M. Scott Ford
Will Rossiter
Zac Williams

Acquisition Editor
Meeta Rajani

Content Development Editor
Athira Laji

Technical Editors
Ankita Jha
Sebastian Rodrigues

Copy Editors
Tanvi Gaitonde
Insiya Morbiwala
Shambhavi Pai
Laxmi Subramanian

Project Coordinators
Melita Lobo
Jomin Varghese

Proofreader
Simran Bhogal

Indexers
Mariammal Chettiyar
Monica Ajmera Mehta

Production Coordinator
Saiprasad Kadam

Cover Work
Saiprasad Kadam

About the Author

Michael Larkin has been building software professionally for over a decade and has worked on large and small projects for companies across the globe. He has been working with Shopify for over five years and has co-created the first ever Shopify app, available at `http://fetchapp.com`. He has also worked on dozens of Shopify stores for which he built custom applications, modified existing themes, and added complex JavaScript to enhance the shopper's experience.

I would like to thank my wife, Sarah, for her help and patience while I was writing this book. I'd also like to thank my colleagues and friends who offered their professional and technical expertise as reviewers. Additionally, I'd like to thank the folks over at Jaded Pixel for creating such an excellent platform. Finally, I'd like to thank Packt Publishing for making all of this possible.

About the Reviewers

Joey deVilla has worked on all sorts of projects, such as creating Olympic athlete training software, CD-ROM directories for every mall in America with Visual Basic, Python-powered gift certificates, travel agency websites, the frontend for the censorship-thwarting project Peekabooty in C++, Duke of URL in PHP that suggests domain names, and a failed social networking app for frat dudes and dudettes in Ruby on Rails. He's also done some technical evangelism for OpenCola, Tucows, Microsoft, and Shopify. He's currently stirring up trouble in the mobile industry, and when he's not doing that, he's stirring up trouble playing Nine Inch Nails, AC/DC, and Britney Spears on his accordion.

> I'd like to thank my family and Anitra for helping me during some really crazy times.

Christophe Favresse developed a passion for e-commerce technologies, and in early 2013, launched his wife's online retail business (www.favresse.com) powered by Shopify and Amazon fulfillment services. In less than one year, this website attracted customers from eight EU countries and the U.S. Christophe, an international sales executive in the software industry, has spent the last 15 years prospecting telecom operators and providing CRM, marketing, and risk assurance solutions to optimize their customer lifetime value and revenues. He has spent two years in Thailand and 15 years in the UK. He currently lives near Nice (France) with his wife and four children. He holds a master's degree in International Marketing from Michael Smurfit School of Business (Ireland) and a bachelor's degree in Economics from Solvay Brussels School (Belgium).

M. Scott Ford has been developing software for the last 15 years. He's worked in many industries, from aerospace to e-commerce. His goal is to stay a polyglot developer. He's worked with many different languages and frameworks over the years, but his favorites are Ruby, JavaScript, and Objective-C.

Scott is the founder of corgibytes (`http://corgibytes.com`), a consulting company with a focus on legacy applications. This is where he applies a pragmatic, test-focused approach to working with existing code. This results in a new life for apps that would otherwise have to be rewritten or abandoned.

Will Rossiter is a Senior Web Developer for DNA Design in New Zealand; he oversees the architecture, development, and maintenance of large-scale web applications across a range of platforms and technologies, including Shopify, WordPress, SilverStripe, Node.js, and Ruby on Rails. He is the creator and maintainer of the grunt-shopify plugin for publishing Shopify themes.

Zac Williams is a Full Stack Web Developer from Birmingham, Alabama with over 10 years of experience. Although he has experience with a variety of frameworks and languages, his specialties are Ruby on Rails and JavaScript. He has experience working on high-traffic web applications across multiple industries, such as e-commerce, healthcare, and higher education.

www.PacktPub.com

Support files, eBooks, discount offers, and more

You might want to visit www.PacktPub.com for support files and downloads related to your book.

Did you know that Packt offers eBook versions of every book published, with PDF and ePub files available? You can upgrade to the eBook version at www.PacktPub.com and as a print book customer, you are entitled to a discount on the eBook copy. Get in touch with us at service@packtpub.com for more details.

At www.PacktPub.com, you can also read a collection of free technical articles, sign up for a range of free newsletters and receive exclusive discounts and offers on Packt books and eBooks.

http://PacktLib.PacktPub.com

Do you need instant solutions to your IT questions? PacktLib is Packt's online digital book library. Here, you can access, read and search across Packt's entire library of books.

Why subscribe?

- Fully searchable across every book published by Packt
- Copy and paste, print and bookmark content
- On demand and accessible via web browser

Free access for Packt account holders

If you have an account with Packt at www.PacktPub.com, you can use this to access PacktLib today and view nine entirely free books. Simply use your login credentials for immediate access.

Table of Contents

Preface

Shopify has grown by leaps and bounds over the last few years and their ever expanding client list means that now is the perfect time to build a killer app to meet the needs of storeowners across the globe. With the release of the App Store, customers can read reviews, see screenshots, and install apps with a few clicks.

There has been a lot of effort from Shopify to make the developer experience as simple as possible. Free software libraries, extensive documentation, and a comprehensive API makes building and launching an app an enjoyable and lucrative process.

This book will teach you how to build an app starting with the setup of your local development environment, installing Ruby, and generating a basic Rails application.

Next, we'll go through several iterations as we build, refactor, and enhance our app, so that you get a feel of development best practices that are currently being used by software companies around the world. We'll wrap up monetizing the app using the Shopify Billing API, which is a simple and PCI-compliant way for us to charge users when they upgrade.

What this book covers

Chapter 1, *Getting Started with Shopify*, covers the basic functionality of Shopify and then explains the difference between private and public apps. A brief overview of the API and webhook systems is provided. The chapter then wraps up with a few thoughts on how to get started with building an app.

Chapter 2, Setting Up, focuses on setting up the reader's development environment, installing Ruby, Rails, and a few other requisite Gems. It shows us how to create a standard Rails site, update it with Twitter Bootstrap, and check it with source control. The chapter wraps up with instructions on how to deploy to Heroku for scalable web hosting.

Chapter 3, Building a Private App, covers the integration with Shopify's API in order to retrieve product and order information from the shop. The UI is then streamlined a bit before the logic to create a contest is created.

Chapter 4, Going Public, shows us how to refactor the existing app to support multiple Shopify accounts simultaneously. It then shows us how to hook into the installation process as well as how to subscribe and process webhooks.

Chapter 5, App Billing and Publication, completes the app by adding a free and paid plan and demonstrates how to setup a recurring charge via the Shopify Billing API. The chapter wraps up by explaining the process for publishing the app in the App Store so that the storeowners can install it automatically.

What you need for this book

You will need a computer capable of running Ruby and a text editor/IDE suitable for developing Rails. A Shopify and a Heroku account are required. It's recommended that an account with a source control service such as GitHub or Bitbucket be used for code management and back up.

Who this book is for

This book is highly suited for Ruby developers who are interested in creating apps for fun and profit. Familiarity with Shopify is helpful but not required. Developers familiar with other web languages should be able to follow but would benefit from a Ruby Primer before reading this book.

Basic command line skills (Windows or Linux) are required as well, but these will be given in a format that can be copied and pasted as needed.

Conventions

In this book, you will find a number of styles of text that distinguish between different kinds of information. Here are some examples of these styles, and an explanation of their meaning.

Code words in text, database table names, folder names, filenames, file extensions, pathnames, dummy URLs, user input, and Twitter handles are shown as follows: "To use Rails 4.0.0 with Heroku, we need to add the `rails_12factor` gem to the Gemfile so that we can precompile our assets."

A block of code is set as follows:

```
def obscure_string(string, count)
    return string if count.blank?
    substring = string.slice(0..(-1 * count - 1))
    return string.gsub(substring, "*" * substring.length)
end
```

When we wish to draw your attention to a particular part of a code block, the relevant lines or items are set in bold:

```
resources :products do
  collection do
    get 'import'
  end
  resources :variants
end
```

Commands that need to be entered at the terminal / shell window are set as follows:

```
gem install rails -v 4.0.0 --no-ri --no-rdoc
```

New terms and **important words** are shown in bold. Words that you see on the screen, in menus or dialog boxes for example, appear in the text like this: "You should see a **Welcome aboard** page that lists out some helpful tips as well as information about the application's configuration as shown in the following screenshot:".

Warnings or important notes appear in a box like this.

Tips and tricks appear like this.

Reader feedback

Feedback from our readers is always welcome. Let us know what you think about this book—what you liked or may have disliked. Reader feedback is important for us to develop titles that you really get the most out of.

To send us general feedback, simply send an e-mail to feedback@packtpub.com, and mention the book title through the subject of your message.

If there is a topic that you have expertise in and you are interested in either writing or contributing to a book, see our author guide on www.packtpub.com/authors.

Customer support

Now that you are the proud owner of a Packt book, we have a number of things to help you to get the most from your purchase.

Downloading the example code

You can download the example code files for all Packt books you have purchased from your account at http://www.packtpub.com. If you purchased this book elsewhere, you can visit http://www.packtpub.com/support and register to have the files e-mailed directly to you. Additionally, the complete source code for the application is available online at http://github.com/mikelarkin/contestapp.

Errata

Although we have taken every care to ensure the accuracy of our content, mistakes do happen. If you find a mistake in one of our books—maybe a mistake in the text or the code—we would be grateful if you would report this to us. By doing so, you can save other readers from frustration and help us improve subsequent versions of this book. If you find any errata, please report them by visiting http://www.packtpub.com/support, selecting your book, clicking on the **errata submission form** link, and entering the details of your errata. Once your errata are verified, your submission will be accepted and the errata will be uploaded to our website, or added to any list of existing errata, under the Errata section of that title.

Piracy

Piracy of copyright material on the Internet is an ongoing problem across all media. At Packt, we take the protection of our copyright and licenses very seriously. If you come across any illegal copies of our works, in any form, on the Internet, please provide us with the location address or website name immediately so that we can pursue a remedy.

Please contact us at copyright@packtpub.com with a link to the suspected pirated material.

We appreciate your help in protecting our authors, and our ability to bring you valuable content.

Questions

You can contact us at questions@packtpub.com if you are having a problem with any aspect of the book, and we will do our best to address it.

1
Getting Started with Shopify

Shopify is a **Software as a Service (SaaS)** e-commerce platform built to meet the needs of the typical storeowner. It offers hosting, shopping cart, payment processing, order management, product catalogs, blogging, and much more. A storeowner can sign up for Shopify, pick out a design, create a product catalog, set up a payment gateway, and make a sale on the same day—all without any programming or technical expertise.

Shopify gives you the ability to completely modify the HTML, CSS, and JavaScript of the storefront theme. Designers are able to add features such as visual effects, responsive designs, bundled products, shipping estimators, and social plugins that can accomplish almost everything that is expected of a modern e-commerce site.

For features such as inventory management, accounting, drop shipping, mailing lists, and, reporting, an application that communicates with Shopify's API and/or handles Shopify's XML notifications (called webhooks) is needed. In this book, we'll focus on building such an app. You should have an understanding of web development using a server-side language such as Ruby, PHP, or ASP.NET. Basic HTML, CSS, and JavaScript skills are also required because we'll be building a simple UI. Finally, familiarity with Shopify's features will be extremely helpful. If you've not used Shopify before, I encourage you to go through this excellent primer on the Shopify blog at `http://www.shopify.com/technology/3671962-developing-shopify-apps-part-1-the-setup`.

Throughout the course of this book, we will be building a web application that allows the storeowners to run contests by randomly picking a customer who has placed an order in the shop. Our app will be built using Ruby on Rails (`http://rubyonrails.org`), which is an open source web development framework that is relatively simple to learn. It is the same language that Shopify has been written in. A few popular Ruby libraries (for example, Active Merchant and Liquid) are extractions of the Shopify source code that have been released as open source. Rails is based on the **Model-View-Controller** (**MVC**) enterprise architecture pattern, so if you aren't familiar with this paradigm, I encourage you to head over to Wikipedia for a general overview (`http://en.wikipedia.org/wiki/Model-view-controller`).

This chapter will cover the following topics:

- An overview of the Shopify platform
- App development options
- The Shopify API
- The Shopify Webhook system
- Tips on how to get started

Revealing Shopify's power

Shopify offers a comprehensive e-commerce solution designed to meet the needs of a typical storeowner who wants to sell products online. The theme gallery, extensive wiki, and active forum provide an excellent end-to-end experience even for the most inexperienced computer user. For customers who need more personalized support, there is the Shopify Experts directory, which is a great place to find a designer, programmer, or setup expert.

Two features, the robust API (`http://docs.shopify.com/api`) and the App Store (`http://apps.shopify.com`), put Shopify ahead of the curve compared to its competitors. Rather than trying to include every imaginable feature for every possible line of business, Shopify focuses on the common needs of every storeowner and leaves the rest to the theme customization and apps.

A third feature called webhooks (`http://docs.shopify.com/api/webhook`) allows apps to receive near real-time notifications of events that take place in a shop. These events range from order creation, product updates, customer signup, to account cancellation. The notifications come in both XML and JSON formats and typical mirror the schema of the API which makes integration a breeze.

Deciding which type of app to build

[handwritten: PRIVATE PUBLIC]

When it comes to building an app for Shopify, there are two options: **private** and **public**. Private applications are designed to access one Shopify store, and can be changed as per the needs of the storeowner by the developer. Public applications are designed to access multiple Shopify stores, and provide functionality that will be used by different types of businesses. They can act as a revenue stream for the developer by charging storeowners a monthly fee.

Both private and public apps perform operations by using the Shopify API and/or by processing Shopify Webhooks. At a high level, a public application can be thought of as a private application that was expanded to work with multiple stores.

To determine which one you need to build, take a look at the following scenarios:

Scenario 1

- You have a client Shopify store that needs additional functionality
- You have already determined that what they need is not included in the Shopify out of the box
- You've looked through the App Store and determined that there isn't an app that meets their needs
- They aren't interested in reselling the idea to other storeowners, or they don't want competitors to have this functionality

 What you are looking to build is a **private app**. This is an app that is not listed in the official App Store and typically only connects to a single Shopify account.

Scenario 2

- You or your client have a great idea for an app
- Other storeowners would benefit from the app and may even pay money to use it

- You've already checked the App Store and determined that the app doesn't already exist, or that it exists but you think you can improve the idea

 What you are looking to build is a **public app**. This is an application that can access multiple stores and that is listed in the App Store. It can be installed automatically by storeowners.

Discovering the API

Shopify offers an extensive API that allows developers to perform almost any task that can be done via the web admin (and a few that don't like working with `Metafields`). The full documentation is available at `http://api.shopify.com`.

The API is RESTful and supports HTTP, JSON, and XML requests. There are several free software libraries available for most of the popular web development languages to help people get started. The libraries are actively supported either by Shopify or the open source community.

In this book, we will only be scratching the surface of the API by focusing on the areas of order retrieval, product management, and application charges. The API allows you to do much more—from modifying the store's themes, setting up shipping charges, to retrieving information about abandoned carts in order to follow up with the shopper.

We'll be working with the following API verticals:

- Application charge
- Product
- Order
- Webhook

Exploring webhooks

Shopify allows applications to subscribe to a series of notifications called webhooks (`http://docs.shopify.com/api/webhook`) around common events such as order placement, product updates, and customer signup. Real-world events are mapped to topics that can be subscribed to via the API or by manual setup in the Shopify admin panel. The webhook notification mirrors the format of the API, which makes the implementation code reusable. When an event occurs, Shopify automatically sends the notification to all subscribers.

[handwritten annotations: "← PUB/SUB QU6U..", "SHOPIFY NOTIFIES"]

Orders

Order webhooks allow apps to respond in a near real-time fashion when an order is placed or updated in the Shopify store. The following two events are the most commonly subscribed topics that deal with the creation and payment of an Order:

- orders/create
- orders/paid

Products

Product webhooks can be handy for apps that handle inventory, product feeds, or back office integrations. The following three events are of interest when dealing with Products:

- products/create
- products/update
- products/delete

Shop/Application

It will be helpful to automatically reflect any updates to a shop's name, URL, and so on in your app. Likewise, it's polite to suspend/cancel a user's account if they uninstall the app from their store. The following two events allow us to do that:

- shop/update
- app/uninstall

Webhooks are sent asynchronously after the event occurs. This makes them suitable for near real-time actions and allows an application to process information in smaller chunks, which can reduce the load and improve performance.

I also recommend using the API to retrieve information as a backup in case the webhook system gets bogged down or a notification is missed.

For public applications, the webhook for uninstalling the application should be subscribed to so that you can automatically suspend the client's account when they remove your app from their Shopify store.

Getting ready to build an app

If you've decided that you need to build an app, then the next step is to ask yourself the following questions:

- What exactly does the app need to do?
- Will the app be private or public?
- Who will be developing the app?
- Who will be designing the UI?
- What is the budget and timeline?

Once you've answered these questions, you should have a rough idea of the big pieces involved in creating the app. The set of features required to build a software is often referred to as the **scope**.

Determining an application's scope even at a high level is a skill that requires practice. This typically starts as a document that lists the overall purpose, feature list, integration points with Shopify (if known), dependencies on external services or software libraries, proprietary business logic, architectural decisions (language, platform, server requirements, and so on), budget, timeframe, and anything else that will impact the application life cycle.

Creating in-depth specs is beyond the scope of this book, though in general more information at this phase is better (it's easier to trim features and defer them at a later phase as development progresses rather than trying to cram in new ones that were forgotten in the beginning).

At the very least, a list of must-have features is necessary. Even if you are doing the development yourself and the feature set is small, it's a good skill to learn and will often reveal aspects and features that weren't originally planned. This is the technique we'll be using throughout this book. We are going to list out the high-level features that we want to build and turn each one into a **sprint**. A sprint is an agile methodology term that denotes a discrete amount of work. Usually, a sprint lasts for two weeks or less. In our case, each sprint will last only a few hours because our feature set is simple.

For a larger app, the simplest way to start is to list out all the features, prioritize them, and then set a cutoff based on time and budget. Even if it never progresses beyond a simple list, you'll have something to measure progress against while the app is being developed. Without this list, all the features (complete and pending) will only be in your head.

An analogy for this would be going to the grocery store without a list. Chances are, most of the things you need will end up in the cart, but undoubtedly, you'll either forget a few things (feature deficiency), spend excess time roaming the aisles trying to remember what you need by seeing something you forgot on the shelf (inefficient development/refactoring), or add things that aren't on the list (scope creep). The worst situation to be in is to have all the ingredients to make lunch tomorrow but be unable to make dinner tonight because you forgot something important!

Summary

In this chapter, we looked at some of the features available in Shopify as well as the difference between private and public applications. Then we briefly discussed the Shopify API and webhook system before finishing up with some thoughts on software development and how to get started planning your own app for fun and profit.

During the course of this book, we will be developing a simple app that will allow storeowners to run contests. The app will pick a winner from the list of customers who have made a purchase at the store within a certain timeframe or for a certain product.

The next chapter will cover setting up your local development environment, installing Ruby on Rails, creating a basic app, and deploying it to Heroku (http://www.heroku.com) for cloud hosting. This application will be iteratively expanded in each chapter as we progress towards our goal of publishing it in the Shopify App Store.

2
Setting Up

The web application that we'll be building throughout the course of the book will be written in Ruby using the open source Rails framework. To quote `http://rubyonrails.org`:

> *"Ruby on Rails® is an open-source web framework that's optimized for programmer happiness and sustainable productivity. It lets you write beautiful code by favoring convention over configuration."*

I couldn't agree more. I find Rails fun to use and the development process to be very intuitive. The community is very active and there are tons of free resources online. It's also worth mentioning that Shopify is written in Rails and many popular Ruby libraries such as Active Merchant and Liquid are extractions of the Shopify source code.

 Although the simplicity of Rails makes it an ideal tool for building our application, we could have just as easily used any web framework, such as ASP.NET, PHP, or Django and achieved a similar result. Remember, the end goal is to output HTML/CSS and JavaScript to the browser as efficiently as possible.

Rails uses the **Model-View-Controller (MVC)** architectural pattern. This pattern facilitates development by creating boundaries between application layers. These boundaries allow concurrent development, multi-level testing, rapid prototyping, and scalability.

Additionally, Rails includes the Active Record pattern that interfaces with common database engines, such as MySQL, PostgreSQL, SQLite, and MS SQL (to name a few) and can be run on Linux, Mac OS X, and Windows. For in-depth explanations of these two patterns, check out *Patterns of Enterprise Application Architecture, Martin Fowler, Pearson Education, Inc.* (`http://www.martinfowler.com/books/eaa.html`).

This chapter will cover the following topics:

- Choosing a development tool
- Setting up our development environment
- Generating a Rails app
- Installing Twitter Bootstrap
- Setting up source control
- Deploying to Heroku

Choosing a development tool

Programmers are as passionate about the tools they use to write code as they are about which language the code is written in. There is typically a trade-off between speed and ease of use, in that the tools that are the fastest tend to require memorization of keystrokes and jargon; whereas the ones that are easier to use sacrifice efficiency for a more intuitive user experience.

There are several options available when developing Rails applications. A couple of popular simpler editors are Sublime Text (`http://www.sublimetext.com`) and TextMate (`http://macromates.com`). A few popular rich editors are RubyMine (`http://www.jetbrains.com/ruby`), Aptana (`http://www.aptana.com`), and Visual Studio with Ruby in Steel (`http://sapphiresteel.com`).

I've tried them all, and personally tend to oscillate between RubyMine and Sublime Text, depending on the project. If I'll be doing a lot of visual debugging, I'll use RubyMine. But for most projects, I find the speed and intuitive features of Sublime Text to be, well, sublime.

 Selecting an editor is a personal choice, and there really isn't a wrong answer. I know developers that still swear by Vim! My only encouragement is to occasionally try out something new; if you don't like it or the learning curve is too steep, you can always revert to your old editor.

In short, there are plenty of excellent options that will help you develop your application efficiently, and it might take trying a few out before you settle on the one you like.

Setting up our development environment

Before we can build our app, we need to set up our local development environment so that we can commit code and deploy to Heroku.

Installing a Ruby management tool

Given the variety of ways in which Ruby can be installed, I would suggest using a Ruby / Gem management tool to handle it for you. The following are a few worth noting:

- The following tools can be used on Mac/Linux PCs:

  - **Ruby Version Manager** (**RVM**) (`https://rvm.io`)

  - Rbenv (`https://github.com/sstephenson/rbenv`)

- The following tool can be used on Windows PCs:

  - Pik (`https://github.com/vertiginous/pik/`)

Even if this is your only Ruby on Rails app, it's good practice to isolate applications from each other to avoid version conflicts or inadvertent software updates on. RVM allows you to not only install and manage multiple versions of Ruby on the same system, but also create **gemsets** which are containers for an application's **gems**. Gems are Ruby libraries that can be used to add common functionality to your app quickly and easily. If you don't use a gemset, Ruby will install everything onto the system's gem container, which means that later versions of the same gems will be installed side by side as you build more apps in the future. This can lead to all sorts of fun dependency loading issues (though to be fair, Bundler handles this quite nicely). It's easier to spend a few minutes and start with isolation so as to avoid the issue altogether.

We'll do everything using the terminal. Sure, there are GUI tools for some of these tasks, but I find that working in a shell on my development machine keeps me in the right mindset when I am working on a Linux production server. So, open up a terminal window and let's get started!

Installing RVM is simple. We need to use the following steps:

1. The following command (the leading slash is intentional) can be used to install RVM:

   ```
   \curl -L https://get.rvm.io | bash -s stable
   ```

   Once the installation is complete, make sure that you look for any additional instructions given at the end of the process. These are typically notes on updating your local bash profile or perhaps installing missing system libraries.

2. You can confirm the installation by checking the version of RVM with the following command:

```
rvm -v
```

The response should look something like the following command:

```
rvm 1.25.25 (stable) by Wayne E. Seguin <wayneeseguin@gmail.com>,
Michal Papis <mpapis@gmail.com> [https://rvm.io/]
```

Installing Ruby

At the time of writing this book, Ruby 2.1.2 had been released and deemed stable. As mentioned, rather than downloading the binaries and installing it ourselves, we'll use RVM. We use the following steps:

1. Run the following command to install Ruby:

```
rvm install 2.1.2
```

2. Once the process is complete, you can confirm the installation by checking the installed version of Ruby by typing the following command:

```
ruby -v
```

The response should look something like the following command:

```
ruby 2.1.2p95 (2014-05-08 revision 45877)
```

Creating the application directory

Now, we need to create the directory for our app, as well as files to let RVM know what version of Ruby to use and which gemset our gems will be stored in. We'll use the following commands for that purpose:

```
mkdir contestapp
cd contestapp
rvm --ruby-version use 2.1.2@contestapp --create
```

Installing Rails

For the purposes of this book, I am going to explicitly specify the version of Rails we want to use rather than just grabbing the latest stable version. I am doing this to ensure that the code examples work correctly several months from now. One catch when using the latest version of Rails is that the gems you want to use might not have been updated yet by their authors. This can lead to bugs being introduced that might not have an easy solution. I tend to lag one version behind (although I do keep an eye out for critical security patches) to ensure that I can build stable apps for my clients. The following command can be used to install Rails 4.0.3:

```
gem install rails -v 4.0.3 --no-ri --no-rdoc
```

Generating a Rails app

Rails comes with many helpful scripts, including one to generate a "vanilla" Rails application as follows:

```
rails new .
```

The preceding command will create the app in the current directory and automatically install the required gems. At this point, we can start up the server with the following command:

```
rails server
```

The response will be similar to the following output:

```
=> Booting WEBrick
=> Rails 4.0.3 application starting in development on http://0.0.0.0:3000
=> Run `rails server -h` for more startup options
=> Ctrl-C to shutdown server
[2014-03-29 21:07:26] INFO  WEBrick 1.3.1
[2014-03-29 21:07:26] INFO  ruby 2.1.1 (2014-02-24) [x86_64-darwin12.0]
[2014-03-29 21:07:26] INFO  WEBrick::HTTPServer#start: pid=14160
port=3000
```

By default, Rails listens to port 3000, so we can view the site by opening up our browser and going to `http://localhost:3000`. You should see a **Welcome aboard** page that lists some helpful tips as well as information about the application's configuration, as shown in the following screenshot:

This page will automatically disappear once we've made our own controllers and views, which is what we're going to do next. Rails provides many helpful scripts to generate code for models, views, controllers, database schema creation, testing frameworks, and much more. To get started, we're going to generate a simple controller and view that will be used as a dashboard for our users. Open up a new terminal window, navigate to the root folder of your app, and use the following command to create a `DashboardController` class that has an `index` action:

```
rails generate controller Dashboard index
```

This command will create several files that we'll modify later on. We'll need to update the `routes` file to make this new action our default. To do this, add the following line to config/routes.rb below the line get "dashboard/index":

```
root 'dashboard#index'
```

If you refresh the browser window instead of the default Rails page, you'll now see a page telling you where the view file for the index action is located, which is shown in the following screenshot. Don't worry; we'll fix the ugliness soon!

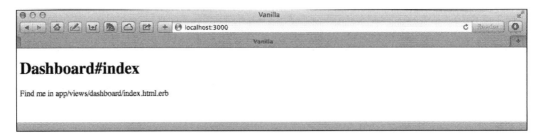

Now that we've completed the *Hello World* equivalent in Rails, it's time to leverage the Twitter Bootstrap framework to improve the UI for us.

Installing Twitter Bootstrap

The official website is `http://getbootstrap.com` and it describes Bootstrap as:

> *"The most popular front-end framework for developing responsive, mobile first projects on the web."*

What this means is that we can use Bootstrap to easily allow our web pages to scale based on the device being used. We no longer have to worry about creating separate view files for phones, tablets, and browsers. The scaling is automatically handled using CSS and JavaScript. Bootstrap also includes helpful CSS styles for making buttons stand out, formatting error messages correctly, and a myriad of other common tasks.

Now, it's time to install Bootstrap using some helpful Gems. Add the following lines below the line gem 'sass-rails', '~> 4.0.0' in your Gemfile::

```
gem "execjs"
gem "twitter-bootstrap-rails"
gem "bootstrap-sass"
```

Downloading the example code

You can download the example code files for all Packt books you have purchased from your account at http://www.packtpub.com. If you purchased this book elsewhere, you can visit http://www.packtpub.com/support and register to have the files e-mailed directly to you. Additionally, the complete source code for the application is available online at http://github.com/mikelarkin/contestapp.

Then, execute the following commands in your terminal window to install the gems, add support for Sass stylesheets, and update your current layout file:

```
bundle install
rails generate bootstrap:install sass
rails g bootstrap:layout application fluid -f
```

The `-f` option automatically overwrites the default `application.html.erb` layout that Rails generated for us earlier. By the way, you can use `fixed` instead of `fluid` if you prefer that layout style.

We need to stop and start our Rails server in order to load Bootstrap. Do this by pressing *CTRL + C* in the terminal window running the Rails server. Then, run the following command to start the app up again:

```
rails server
```

Once that's done, we can then reload our browser window and see the results. If we adjust the browser width, the elements on the page automatically scale to fit. We'll worry about updating the sidebar and navigation in the next chapter as we dive into building the application.

Setting up source control

At this point, it's a good idea to add our code to a hosted source control. This serves two purposes: the first is that it gives us a record of incremental changes made to each code file, and also acts as an off-site backup in case our development machine gets damaged or has a hard drive failure.

We'll be using Git (`http://git-scm.com`) as our **Source Control Management (SCM)** tool. If you don't have Git installed on your system, please follow the relevant installation instructions on the site. Additionally, we're going to use GitHub (`http://github.com`) as our off-site backup. There are other popular alternatives such as Bitbucket (`http://bitbucket.org`) or Unfuddle (`http://unfuddle.com`) that work just as well.

The workflow may vary depending on which service you use, but in general setting up a new repository involves the following steps:

1. Create a repository on the hosted service of your choice.
2. Initialize a new local repository using the following command:
    ```
    git init.
    ```
3. Add a remote reference to the online service using the next command:
    ```
    git remote add origin <path_to_remote_repository>
    ```
4. Add any existing files to the repository and create a commit using the following commands:
    ```
    git add --all
    git commit -am "Initial commit"
    ```
5. Push the changes upstream to the hosted service with the following command:
    ```
    git push -u origin master
    ```

Once you've completed the initial setup, subsequent commits need to be done at regular intervals to ensure that work isn't lost.

Deploying to Heroku

Heroku (`http://heroku.com`) is a polyglot **Platform as a Service (PaaS)** that allows scalable hosting of websites written in several popular languages, including Ruby, Python, and Java. Deployment is as simple as installing the Heroku toolbelt and running a few commands. Heroku keeps a copy of our code on its own Git server and deploys the latest version when we do a `push`.

Sign up for Heroku and then head over to `https://toolbelt.heroku.com` and follow the installation instructions for your OS.

 If you use **Apache Subversion (SVN)** or **Concurrent Versions System (CVS)** instead of Git, please note that you'll need to also use Git as it is required for deployment to Heroku: `https://devcenter.heroku.com/articles/git#using-subversion-or-other-revision-control-systems`.

We need to perform the following steps while using Heroku:

1. To use Rails 4.0.3 with Heroku, we need to add the `rails_12factor` gem to the Gemfile so that we can precompile our assets.

   By default, Rails compiles the JavaScript and CSS assets on the first page load after deployment, and saves them to the disk to be cached. However, Heroku uses a read-only filesystem, and will not allow the compiled files to be permanently saved.

   Also, Heroku uses PostgreSQL exclusively, so we'll need to add the `pg` gem to our Gemfile. Finally, we need to tell Heroku which version of Ruby we want to use to ensure that we get the correct stack each time we deploy. Add the following lines to your Gemfile under the `gem 'rails', '4.0.3'` line:

   ```
   ruby 2.1.2
   group :production do
     gem "rails_12factor"
     gem "pg"
   end
   ```

   We need to wrap the `sqlite3` gem into a nonproduction group as well so that it doesn't get deployed to Heroku, using the following lines:

   ```
   group :development, :test do
     gem "sqlite3"
   end
   ```

2. And then update the bundle with the following command:

   ```
   bundle install
   ```

3. Let's commit these updates and push them to GitHub using the following commands:

   ```
   git add --all
   git commit -am "Required Heroku gems"
   git push
   ```

4. The next step is to create the app on Heroku, deploy our code, and build the database using the following commands:

   ```
   heroku create contestapp
   git push heroku master
   heroku run rake db:migrate
   ```

5. Once the migrations have finished running, we can view the site in our default browser by using the following toolbelt shortcut:

   ```
   heroku open
   ```

Summary

In this chapter, we covered a brief overview of the Ruby on Rails platform, looked at different coding tools, got our development environment set up, and started building our application. We decided to use the Twitter Bootstrap framework to make our views responsive and reduce our frontend coding time. Finally, we checked everything into source control and deployed it to Heroku, which is a scalable cloud service that makes hosting Rails sites a breeze.

We now have a functioning website that we can expand to create our contest application. We'll be developing using an iterative approach, with regular commits to source control and deployments to Heroku to keep our production environment up to date.

In the next chapter, we will start with a high-level overview of the application, build the core business logic, and connect it privately to a Shopify test store.

Building a Private App

3

We will be expanding the application we started in the previous chapter to include the ability to organize simple contests and select a winner. It'll start out as a private application tied to a development Shopify account. Later on, we'll refactor the code to support multiple shops and publish it in the Shopify App Store.

Even though the app will be simple and only take a few hours to build, we'll still use good development practices to ensure we create a solid foundation. There are many different approaches to software development and discussing even a fraction of them is beyond the scope of this book. Instead, we'll use a few common concepts, such as requirements gathering, milestones, **Test-Driven Development** (**TDD**), frequent code check-ins, and appropriate commenting/documentation. Personal discipline in following development procedures is one of the best things a developer can bring to a project; it is even more important than writing code.

This chapter will cover the following topics:

- The structure of the app we'll be building
- The development process
- Working with the Shopify API
- Using source control
- Deploying to production

Signing up for Shopify

Before we dive back into code, it would be helpful to get the task of setting up a Shopify store out of the way. Sign up as a Shopify partner by going to `http://partners.shopify.com`. The benefit of this is that partners can provision stores that can be used for testing. Go ahead and make one now before reading further. Keep your login information close at hand; we'll need it in just a moment.

Understanding our workflow

The general workflow for developing our application is as follows:

1. Pull down the latest version of the `master` branch.
2. Pick a feature to implement from our requirements list.
3. Create a topic branch to keep our changes isolated.
4. Write tests that describe the behavior desired by our feature.
5. Develop the code until it passes all the tests.
6. Commit and push the code into the remote repository.
7. Pull down the latest version of the `master` branch and merge it with our topic branch.
8. Run the test suite to ensure that everything still works.
9. Merge the code back with the `master` branch.
10. Commit and push the code to the remote repository.

The previous list should give you a rough idea of what is involved in a typical software project involving multiple developers. The use of topic branches ensures that our work in progress won't affect other developers (called breaking the build) until we've confirmed that our code has passed all the tests and resolved any conflicts by merging in the latest stable code from the `master` branch.

The practical upside of this methodology is that it allows bug fixes or work from another developer to be added to the project at any time without us having to worry about incomplete code polluting the build. This also gives us the ability to deploy production from a stable code base.

In practice, a lot of projects will also have a production branch (or tagged release) that contains a copy of the code currently running in production. This is primarily in case of a server failure so that the application can be restored without having to worry about new features being released ahead of schedule, and secondly so that if a new deploy introduces bugs, it can easily be rolled back.

Building the application

We'll be building an application that allows Shopify storeowners to organize contests for their shoppers and randomly select a winner. Contests can be configured based on purchase history and timeframe. For example, a contest could be organized for all the customers who bought the newest widget within the last three days, or anyone who has made an order for any product in the month of August. To accomplish this, we'll need to be able to pull down order information from the Shopify store, generate a random winner, and show the storeowner the results.

Let's start out by creating a list of requirements for our application. We'll use this list to break our development into discrete pieces so we can easily measure our progress and also keep our focus on the important features. Of course, it's difficult to make a complete list of all the requirements and have it stick throughout the development process, which is why a common strategy is to develop in iterations (or sprints). The result of an iteration is a working app that can be reviewed by the client so that the remaining features can be reprioritized if necessary.

High-level requirements

The requirements list comprises all the tasks we're going to accomplish in this chapter. The end result will be an application that we can use to run a contest for a single Shopify store. Included in the following list are any related database, business logic, and user interface coding necessary.

1. Install a few necessary gems.
2. Store Shopify API credentials.
3. Connect to Shopify.
4. Retrieve order information from Shopify.
5. Retrieve product information from Shopify.
6. Clean up the UI.
7. Pick a winner from a list.
8. Create contests.

Now that we have a list of requirements, we can treat each one as a sprint. We will work in a topic branch and merge our code to the `master` branch at the end of the sprint.

Installing a few necessary gems

The first item on our list is to add a few code libraries (gems) to our application. Let's create a topic branch and do just that. To avoid confusion over which branch contains code for which feature, we can start the branch name with the requirement number. We'll additionally prepend the chapter number for clarity, so our format will be `<chapter #>_<requirement #>_<branch name>`. Execute the following command line in the root folder of the app:

```
git checkout -b ch03_01_gem_updates
```

This command will create a local branch called `ch03_01_gem_updates` that we will use to isolate our code for this feature. Once we've installed all the gems and verified that the application runs correctly, we'll merge our code back with the `master` branch.

At a minimum we need to install the gems we want to use for testing. For this app we'll use **RSpec**. We'll need to use the development and test group to make sure the testing gems aren't loaded in production.

1. Add the following code in bold to the block present in the Gemfile that we created in the last chapter:

```
group :development, :test do

  gem "sqlite3"
  # Helpful gems
  gem "better_errors" # improves error handling
  gem "binding_of_caller" # used by better errors

  # Testing frameworks
  gem 'rspec-rails' # testing framework
  gem "factory_girl_rails" # use factories, not fixtures
  gem "capybara" # simulate browser activity
  gem "fakeweb"

  # Automated testing
  gem 'guard' # automated execution of test suite upon change
  gem "guard-rspec" # guard integration with rspec

  # Only install the rb-fsevent gem if on Max OSX
  gem 'rb-fsevent' # used for Growl notifications

end
```

2. Now we need to head over to the terminal and install the gems via Bundler with the following command:

```
bundle install
```

3. The next step is to install RSpec:

```
rails generate rspec:install
```

4. The final step is to initialize Guard:

```
guard init rspec
```

This will create a Guard file, and fill it with the default code needed to detect the file changes.

5. We can now restart our Rails server and verify that everything works properly. We have to do a full restart to ensure that any initialization files are properly picked up. Once we've ensured that our page loads without issue, we can commit our code and merge it back with the `master` branch:

```
git add --all
git commit -am "Added gems for testing"
git checkout master
git merge ch03_01_gem_updates
git push
```

Great! We've completed our first requirement.

Storing Shopify API credentials

In order to access our test store's API, we'll need to create a **Private App** and store the provided credentials there for future use. Fortunately, Shopify makes this easy for us via the Admin UI:

1. Go to the **Apps** page.

2. At the bottom of the page, click on the **Create a private API key...** link.

3. Click on the **Generate new Private App** button.

   We'll now be provided with three important pieces of information: the API Key, password, and shared secret. In addition, we can see from the example URL field that we need to track our Shopify URL as well.

4. Now that we have credentials to programmatically access our Shopify store, we can save this in our application. Let's create a topic branch and get to work:

   ```
   git checkout -b ch03_02_shopify_credentials
   ```

5. Rails offers a generator called a **scaffold** that will create the database migration model, controller, view files, and test stubs for us. Run the following from the command line to create the scaffold for the Account vertical (make sure it is all on one line):

   ```
   rails g scaffold Account shopify_account_url:string
   shopify_api_key:string shopify_password:string
   shopify_shared_secret:string
   ```

6. We'll need to run the database migration to create the database table using the following commands:

   ```
   bundle exec rake db:migrate
   bundle exec rake db:migrate RAILS_ENV=test
   ```

7. Use the following command to update the generated view files to make them bootstrap compatible:

```
rails g bootstrap:themed Accounts -f
```

8. Head over to `http://localhost:3000/accounts` and create a new account in our app that uses the Shopify information from the Private App page. By the way, we'll be refactoring this part of the application in the next chapter to make it more secure and user friendly.

9. It's worth getting Guard to run our test suite every time we make a change so we can ensure that we don't break anything. Open up a new terminal in the root folder of the app and start up Guard:

```
bundle exec guard
```

After booting up, Guard will automatically run all our tests. They should all pass because we haven't made any changes to the generated code. If they don't, you'll need to spend time sorting out any failures before continuing.

The next step is to make the app more user friendly. We'll make a few changes now and leave the rest for you to do later.

1. Update the layout file so it has accurate navigation. Boostrap created several dummy links in the header navigation and sidebar. Update the navigation list in `/app/views/layouts/application.html.erb` to include the following code:

```
<a class="brand" href="/">Contestapp</a>
<div class="container-fluid nav-collapse">
  <ul class="nav">
    <li><%= link_to "Accounts", accounts_path%></li>
  </ul>
</div><!--/.nav-collapse -->
```

2. Add validations to the account model to ensure that all fields are required when creating/updating an account. Add the following lines to `/app/models/account.rb`:

```
validates_presence_of :shopify_account_url
validates_presence_of :shopify_api_key
validates_presence_of :shopify_password
validates_presence_of :shopify_shared_secret
```

This will immediately cause the controller tests to fail due to the fact that it is not passing in all the required fields when attempting to submit the created form.

3. If you look at the top of the file, you'll see some code that creates the :valid_attributes hash. If you read the comment above it, you'll see that we need to update the hash to contain the following minimally required fields:

```
# This should return the minimal set of attributes required
# to create a valid Account. As you add validations to
# Account, be sure to adjust the attributes here as well.
let(:valid_attributes) { { "shopify_account_url" =>
"MyString", "shopify_password" => "MyString",
"shopify_api_key" => "MyString", "shopify_shared_secret" =>
"MyString" } }
```

This is a prime example of why having a testing suite is important. It keeps us from writing code that breaks other parts of the application, or in this case, helps us discover a weakness we might not have known we had: the ability to create a new account record without filling in any fields!

4. Now that we have satisfied this requirement and all our tests pass, we can commit the code and merge it with the master branch:

```
git add --all
git commit -am "Account model and related files"
git checkout master
git merge ch03_02_shopify_credentials
git push
```

Excellent! We've now completed another critical piece!

Connecting to Shopify

Now that we have a test store to work with, we're ready to implement the code necessary to connect our app to Shopify.

1. First, we need to create a topic branch:

```
git checkout -b ch03_03_shopify_connection
```

2. We are going to use the official Shopify gem to connect our app to our test store, as well as interact with the API. Add this to the Gemfile under the gem 'bootstrap-sass' line:

```
gem 'shopify_api'
```

3. Update the bundle from the command line:

```
bundle install
```

We'll also need to restart Guard in order for it to pick up the new gem. This is typically done by using a key combination like *Ctrl* + *Z* (Windows) or *Cmd* + *C* (Mac OS X) or by typing the word exit and pressing the *Enter* key.

I've written a class that encapsulates the Shopify connection logic and initializes the global `ShopifyAPI` class that we can then use to interact with the API. You can find the code for this class in `ch03_shopify_integration.rb`. You'll need to copy the contents of this file to your app in a new file located at `/app/services/shopify_integration.rb`. The contents of the spec file `ch03_shopify_integration_spec.rb` need to be pasted in a new file located at `/spec/services/shopify_integration_spec.rb`. Using this class will allow us to execute something like `ShopifyAPI::Order.find(:all)` to get a list of orders, or `ShopifyAPI::Product.find(1234)` to retrieve the product with the ID `1234`.

 The spec file contains tests for functionality that we haven't built yet and will initially fail. We'll fix this soon!

We are going to add a **Test Connection** button to the account page that will give the user instant feedback as to whether or not the credentials are valid. Because we will be adding a new action to our application, we will need to first update controller, request, routing, and view tests before proceeding. Given the nature of this book and because in this case, we're connecting to an external service, the topics such as mocking, test writing, and so on will have to be reviewed as homework. I recommend watching the excellent screencasts created by Ryan Bates at `http://railscasts.com` as a primer on testing in Rails.

I'll be showing examples of test code throughout the following chapters; this just happens to be the kind of multilayer, cross-service testing that deserves its own book!

1. The first step is to update the `resources :accounts` route in the `/config/routes.rb` file with the following block:

```
resources :accounts do
    member do
      get 'test_connection'
    end
end
```

2. Copy the controller code from `ch03_accounts_controller.rb` and replace the code in `/app/controllers/accounts_controller.rb` file. This new code adds the `test_connection` method as well as ensuring the account is loaded properly.

3. Finally, we need to add a button to `/app/views/account/show.html.erb` that will call this action in `div.form-actions`:

```
<%= link_to "Test Connection",
test_connection_account_path(@account), :class => 'btn' %>
```

4. If we view the account page in our browser, we can now test our Shopify integration. Assuming that everything was copied correctly, we should see a success message after clicking on the **Test Connection** button. If everything was not copied correctly, we'll see the message that the Shopify API returned to us as a clue to what isn't working.

5. Once all the tests pass, we can commit the code and merge it with the `master` branch:

```
git add --all

git commit -am "Shopify connection and related UI"

git checkout master

git merge ch03_03_shopify_connection

git push
```

Having fun? Good, because things are about to get heavy.

Retrieving product information from Shopify

In order for the contests to be set up based on a product purchase, we need to store product information locally in the application. For now, we'll pull this data in via the API, but another strategy would be to subscribe to product-related webhooks to keep our application in sync automatically.

Let's create a topic branch:

```
git checkout -b ch03_04_product_import
```

Shopify uses variants to handle product options. For example, if the product is a t-shirt, the variants might correspond to the different size options. Each variant can have a different price, SKU, and barcode.

1. To properly store product information in our app, we'll need to create a product model and a variant model. Use the following commands to do just that:

```
rails g scaffold Product name:string
shopify_product_id:integer last_shopify_sync:datetime

rails g scaffold Variant product_id:integer:index
shopify_variant_id:integer option1:string option2:string
option3:string sku:string barcode:string price:float
last_shopify_sync:datetime
```

2. Next, we need to run the migrations to create the tables:

```
bundle exec rake db:migrate

bundle exec rake db:migrate RAILS_ENV=test
```

3. Update the UI to make it Bootstrap compatible:

```
rails g bootstrap:themed Products -f
rails g bootstrap:themed Variants -f
```

4. Restart Guard and then add another navigation link to /app/views/layouts/application.html.erb that points to the order index page:

```
<ul class="nav">
  <li><%= link_to "Products", products_path %></li>
  <li><%= link_to "Accounts", accounts_path %></li>
</ul>
```

5. Next, we need to set up the relationship between products and variants. To do this, we're going to modify the product model (/app/models/product.rb):

```
class Product < ActiveRecord::Base
    has_many :variants
end
```

We are going to also modify the variant model (/app/models/variant.rb) in a similar fashion:

```
class Variant < ActiveRecord::Base
    belongs_to :product
end
```

The previous statements tell Rails how the models are related. In our case, a product is the parent and can have one or more variants associated with it. Likewise, a variant is considered to be a child and can only belong to a single product. This setup allows us to execute something like product.variants or variant.product to reference the related information.

6. The next step is to update the routing to reflect the nested relationship. Update /tests/routing/variants_routing_spec.rb with the code from ch03_variants_routing_spec.rb.

7. As you can see, the tests immediately fail because the default scaffold generator didn't take the nested relationship into account. Head over to /config/routes.rb and move the variant resource inside the product resource:

```
resources :products do
  resources :variants
end
```

This tells Rails that variants can only be accessed in the context of their parent product, which is exactly what we want.

8. The `VariantsController` (`/app/controllers/variants_controller.rb`) class will also need to be updated to automatically load the product specified in the route into the `@product` instance variable. To do this, we are going to add a method called `set_product` and invoke it via a `before_action`:

```
class VariantsController < ApplicationController
  before_action :set_product
  before_action :set_variant, only: [:show, :edit, :update,
:destroy]
```

9. Then, at the bottom of the file, update the private methods:

```
private
  def set_product
    @product = Product.find(params[:product_id])
  end

  def set_variant
    @variant = @product.variants.find(params[:id])
  end
```

Notice that we also modified the `set_variant` method to scope it to `@product.variants` for security purposes. This ensures that another product's variants can't be accidentally (or maliciously) accessed by typing in a different `:id` in the browser address bar.

The rest of the failed tests are also a result of the routing update we just made because now the variant tests need to include the related product. I'll leave these as homework for you to sort out, which will give you further insight into how Rails handles nested resources.

On a project like this where we start building from the bottom up, it's tough to accurately predict what the view tests need to test because the UI isn't finalized. So, keeping them up to date might waste valuable time since the UI is likely to change several times as we add more functionality to the app. In practice, I've often had to mark them as pending until the designs were finalized.

If you aren't a designer yourself, I highly recommend hiring one to provide you with not only the design for your site, but also HTML and CSS used in the view files. This will reduce your development time and give you a visual goal to work towards.

Once the routing and controller logic has been updated, we need to expand our `ShopifyIntegration` class to retrieve product information. Shopify's API returns paginated results, so we'll need to keep that in mind while writing our code. Take a look at the the `import_products` method in `/app/services/shopify_integration.rb` that we copied over earlier. This method iterates through the shop's product catalog and syncs it with our app. This step is necessary because we'll need to use the products and variants in order to organize contests.

The final step is to add a button to the UI that allows a product import to be executed as needed by the storeowner. Even though we'll automate the import once the app is in production, it's a nice touch and doesn't require much work on our end.

1. The first step is to add a route for the import. As usual, we'll update `/spec/routing/product_routing_spec.rb` first by adding the following lines:

    ```
    # Custom Actions
    it "routes to #import" do
      get("/products/import").should route_to("products#import")
    end
    ```

2. Update the products route in `/config/routes.rb` to include the new import route:

    ```
    resources :products do
      collection do
        get 'import'
      end
      resources :variants
    end
    ```

3. Now we need to add the controller action to `/app/controllers/products_controller.rb`:

    ```
    # GET /products/import
    # GET /products/import.json
      def import
      # For now we'll use the first Account in the database
        account = Account.first

      # Instantiate the ShopifyIntegration class
        shopify_integration = ShopifyIntegration.new(
        api_key: account.shopify_api_key,
        shared_secret: account.shopify_shared_secret,
        url: account.shopify_account_url,
        password: account.shopify_password)

        respond_to do |format|
          shopify_integration.connect
    ```

```
          result = shopify_integration.import_products
          format.html { redirect_to ({action: :index}),
          notice: "#{result[:created].to_i} created,
#{result[:updated]}
          updated, #{result[:failed]} failed." }
      end
    end
```

This method connects to Shopify and runs an import. Further work is needed to ensure that the account exists, has proper credentials, responds to JSON, and so on; however, for the sake of space, we'll focus on the key functionality for now.

4. Finally, we need to add a link to the UI. Right now, let's put it under the page header in /app/views/products/index.html.erb:

```
<div class="page-header">
  <h1><%=t '.title', :default =>
  model_class.model_name.human.pluralize.titleize %></h1>
  <p><a href="<%= import_products_path %>">Import Products</a></p>
</div>
```

5. If you open the products page on your browser and click on the **Import Products** link, you should see your products come in from Shopify. Neat, right?

6. As usual, once our tests pass we can commit and merge our code with the master branch using the following commands:

```
git add --all

git commit -am "Shopify Product Import"

git checkout master

git merge ch03_04_product_import

git push
```

Whew! That was a big piece of code. Fortunately, we can reuse a lot of it for the next requirement.

Retrieving order information from Shopify

We are going to save the order information locally in the application's database as well. This will allow us to efficiently organize contests by filtering the data in ways that the Shopify API doesn't provide natively. In the future, we could look into subscribing to webhook notifications to automatically keep our database in sync, but for now, we'll have to check for new orders each time before organizing a contest.

As usual, let's create a topic branch before getting to work:

```
git checkout -b ch03_05_order_import
```

We need to create a table to store order information from Shopify. This will actually require us to make two models: `Order` and `OrderItem`.

1. We'll again use the handy scaffold generator in Rails for the `Order` class and the model generator for `OrderItem`:

   ```
   rails g scaffold Order number:string email:string
   first_name:string last_name:string shopify_order_id:integer
   order_date:datetime total:float line_item_count:integer
   financial_status:string
   ```

   ```
   rails g model OrderItem order_id:integer:index
   variant_id:integer:index shopify_product_id:integer:integer
   shopify_variant_id:integer:index unit_price:float
   quantity:integer
   ```

2. Next, we need to run the migrations to create the tables:

   ```
   bundle exec rake db:migrate
   ```

   ```
   bundle exec rake db:migrate RAILS_ENV=test
   ```

3. Next, we need to set up the relationship between orders and order items. To do this, we're going to modify the product model (/`app/models/order.rb`):

   ```
   class Order < ActiveRecord::Base
           has_many :order_items
   end
   ```

   We are going to also modify the order item model (/`app/models/order_item.rb`) in a similar fashion:

   ```
   class OrderItem < ActiveRecord::Base
           belongs_to :order
   end
   ```

   This setup allows us to execute something like `order.order_items` or `order_item.order` to reference the related information.

4. Use the following command to update the UI to make it Bootstrap compatible:

   ```
   rails g bootstrap:themed Orders -f
   ```

5. Finally, add another navigation link to /`app/views/layouts/application.html.erb` that points to the order index page:

   ```
   <ul class="nav">
     <li><%= link_to "Products", products_path  %></li>
     <li><%= link_to "Orders", orders_path  %></li>
     <li><%= link_to "Accounts", accounts_path  %></li>
   </ul>
   ```

Feel free to make any tweaks to the UI that you want; just be sure to update the relevant tests when you do so.

Go back to the `ShopifyIntegration` class and look at the `import_orders` method. We're going to use this to pull the order information from Shopify. The structure is very similar to `import_products` in that it iterates through the shop's orders and checks to see whether or not it has already been imported. If it has not been imported, the method then creates a new order and related order items. The UI tasks are similar to the product import feature we just added, so we can borrow the code and make the appropriate updates to `/config/routes.rb`, `/app/controllers/orders_controller.rb`, `/app/views/orders/index.html.rb`, and the related tests. Go ahead and make these updates on your own (or look at the files included with the book).

One thing we should consider is executing a product import prior to running the order import. It doesn't make sense for an order to fail to import just because our app doesn't have the product information imported. In the interest of keeping functionality isolated, we won't chain these together, but rather have the controller perform the product import by invoking both methods.

As you probably guessed, once all the tests pass, we can commit the code and merge it with the `master` branch:

```
git add --all
git commit -am "Shopify connection and related UI"
git checkout master
git merge ch03_05_order_import
git push
```

Our integration with Shopify is complete! It's time to take care of a few administrative tasks in preparation of building the contest piece.

Cleaning up the UI

Let's clean up the UI a bit before diving into the contest functionality. The Rails scaffold generator and the Bootstrap scaffolding were extremely helpful in getting us started, so we could focus on the business logic, but it's time for an overhaul.

In particular, we need to clean up / tweak the following areas to hide superfluous information, mask sensitive fields, and otherwise streamline things to make them more user friendly.

As usual, let's create a topic branch before getting to work:

```
git checkout -b ch03_06_ui_cleanup
```

Updating the sidebar

Bootstrap gave us both a top navigation and a sidebar. Though the sidebar is populated with links by default, it also creates place to provide contextual instructions for the page.

We are going to make the content dynamic by using content areas in our view files. This will allow us to not only dynamically render HTML based on the page, but also change the structure of the page to handle cases where no sidebar is needed.

The first thing to do is update /app/views/layouts/application.html.erb to wrap the page content area in a conditional statement:

```
<div class="row-fluid">
  <% if content_for?(:sidebar) %>
  <div class="span3">
    <div class="well sidebar-nav">
      <%= yield(:sidebar) %>
    </div>
  </div>
  <div class="span9">
    <%= bootstrap_flash %>
      <%= yield %>
  </div>
  <% else %>
    <div class="span12">
      <%= bootstrap_flash %>
        <%= yield %>
    </div>
  <% end %>
</div>
```

What this logic does is determine whether or not there is any content for the sidebar using the content_for? helper, and if there is sidebar content, it renders it in a special div. If there is no sidebar content, the wrapper class is changed to span12 so that it takes up the entire width of the page.

We'll now add a sidebar for the dashboard that contains a message. Place the following block at the top of /apps/views/dashboard/index.html.erb:

```
<%- content_for :sidebar do-%>
    <h4>Welcome!</h4>
    <p>This is the Dashboard for your account.  You'll be able to
  view past contest results, as well as create new ones.</p>
<%- end -%>
```

As you can see, we are using the `content_for` block to designate the content that should be inserted in the layout where `:sidebar_key` is referenced. If you refresh the dashboard page on your browser, you'll see our message pop up in the sidebar. If you then browse to the orders page, you'll see that the table now takes up the whole page because no sidebar was provided.

Updating orders, products, and variants

By default, the scaffolding of the `index` page displays every column of the model, which is unnecessary. We'll use the order pages as an example. It makes sense to hide columns such as `shopify_order_id`, `created_at`, and `financial_status`. Furthermore, we could enhance the page to make the number a link that takes us to the `show` page, turn the email address into a `mail_to` link, format the order date, and add a currency symbol next to the total.

We should make similar updates on the `show` page and also turn `shopify_order_id` into a link to the order page in the Shopify store admin. Additionally, the `create` and `edit` forms should be modified to include date pickers, inline validators for e-mail addresses, tooltips, and so on. We also need to display a list of `OrderItems` on the `show` page. Feel free to tinker around with the site and try to add some of these features as homework.

Cleaning up the rest of the site

As mentioned, this sort of UI work is beyond the scope of this book, but it's still a great way to get instant feedback and see visual progress. Just don't forget to update the tests! Once you are satisfied with the UI for the site and have updated any related tests, it's time to commit our work and merge it with the `master` branch:

```
git add --all
git commit -am "UI cleanup"
git checkout master
git merge ch03_06_ui_cleanup
git push
```

Picking a winner from a list

We plan on allowing several types of contests to be configured, so it makes sense to have a common method that takes in a list of contestants as input and randomly picks one. This list will be in the form of an array of IDs, and the result will be the winning ID.

We're going to create another service object with a method that accepts an array and returns a random item. We should also support the ability to pick more than one winner. The `Array#sample` method in Ruby does just that, so all we need to do is wrap a call to this method in our code so that we can ensure consistent results.

The expected functionality boils down to a few simple requirements as follows:

- We need to provide an array of contestants
- If one winner is required, then we will return a single contestant
- If more than one winner is required, then we will return an array of contestants

We're going to complete this task fairly quickly using the following steps:

1. As usual, create a topic branch for this feature:

   ```
   git checkout -b ch03_07_winner_selection
   ```

2. Stub out the class file /app/services/contest_results.rb:

   ```
   class ContestResults
     def initialize(array)
     end

     #Picks <count> winners
       def results(count=1)
       end
   end
   ```

3. Create the test in /spec/services/contest_results_spec.rb:

   ```
   describe ContestResults do
     context "initialize" do
       it "should raise exception if not an array" do
         expect {ContestResults.new([1])}.to_not raise_error
         expect {ContestResults.new([1,2,3,4])}.to_not raise_error
         expect {ContestResults.new(["a","b"])}.to_not raise_error
         expect {ContestResults.new("")}.to raise_error
         expect {ContestResults.new(nil)}.to raise_error
         expect {ContestResults.new([])}.to raise_error
         expect {ContestResults.new}.to raise_error
       end
     end

     context "results" do
       it "should return the proper results" do
         contest_results = ContestResults.new([1,2,3,4])
         contest_results.results.should be_a Integer
   ```

```
contest_results.results(1).should be_a Integer
contest_results.results(2).should be_a Array
contest_results.results(0).should be_a Integer
contest_results.results(nil).should be_a Integer

contest_results = ContestResults.new(["a","b","c","d"])
contest_results.results.should be_a String
contest_results.results(1).should be_a String
contest_results.results(2).should be_a Array
contest_results.results(0).should be_a String
contest_results.results(nil).should be_a String
      end
    end
  end
```

4. Now that we have tests, we can fill in the methods we stubbed out earlier with code. As mentioned, we are going to use the `Array#sample` method and return the results. If we later decide to use a different algorithm to choose a winner, we only need to make the change in one class, and we already have tests in place that will ensure that we don't break existing code elsewhere in the app:

```
class ContestResults
  def initialize(array)
    raise ArgumentError.new("array is required") if array.blank?
    @array = array
  end

  #Picks <count> winners
  def results(count=1)
    if count.to_i < 2
      @array.sample
    else
      @array.sample(count)
    end
  end
end
```

After copying in this code and saving the file, Guard will automatically rerun the tests, which will now pass. This requirement ended up being a quick one to satisfy, which was a nice change. Let's commit the results and tackle the final few tasks on our list:

```
git add --all
git commit -am "Random winner selection"
git checkout master
git merge ch03_07_winner_selection
git push
```

Though we could have done this as part of the contest requirement, it made sense to break it out as a separate task so that the feature can be kept modular and agnostic and to give us room to easily expand the app in the future to organize additional contests based on new criteria.

Creating contests

The ability to run contests is the whole goal of the application. It took a lot of groundwork, but we are ready to add this final piece! For now, we are going to start out by offering the ability to run a couple of different contests:

- Pick a winner from any past purchasers, with or without a date range
- Pick a winner based on a particular product purchase, with or without a date range

Rather than creating a new set of pages for contests, we already have a dashboard page where we can place the list of past contests as well as the form to run a new one. This time we're going to switch things up a bit and create the UI first. This will give us a taste of working from the top down rather than the bottom up. Let's create a topic branch:

```
git checkout -b ch03_08_contests
```

First, we're going to add a form to the dashboard sidebar; we can borrow the structure and the CSS classes from the `Orders` form, and for now, we'll substitute plain HTML with sample values:

1. Replace the sidebar code in `/app/views/dashboard/index.html.erb` with the following:

```
<%- content_for :sidebar do -%>
<h4>New Contest</h4>
<p>Use the form below to run a new Contest. Fields marked
  with * are required.</p>
  <form>
    <div class="control-group">
      <label for="name">Contest Name *</label>
      <div class="controls">
        <input type="text" class="text_field" id="name"
class="name" required/>
      </div>
    </div>
    <div class="control-group">
      <label for="name">Type *</label>
      <div class="controls">
        <select id="product" name="product" required>
```

```
            <option>Any Product</option>
            <optgroup label="Specific Product">
              <option>Product A</option>
              <option>Product B</option>
            </optgroup>
          </select>
        </div>
      </div>
      <div class="control-group">
        <label for="name">Order Date Range (optional)</label>
        <div class="controls">
          <input type="text" class="text_field" id="from-
          date" name="from-date"/> to
          <input type="text" class="text_field" id="to-date"
          name="to-date"/>
        </div>
      </div>
      <div class="control-group">
        <label for="name">Max # (optional)</label>
        <div class="controls">
          <input type="text" class="text_field" id="limit"
          name="limit"/>
        </div>
      </div>
      <div class="form-actions">
        <input type="submit" value="Submit" class="btn"/>
        <%= link_to t('.cancel', :default =>
        t("helpers.links.cancel")),
        dashboard_index_path, :class => 'btn' %>
      </div>
    </form>
<%- end -%>
```

2. Next, we'll copy the HTML table structure from the **Orders** index page to /app/views/dashboard/index.html.erb and replace the `<h1>Dashboard#index</h1><p>Find me in /app/views/dashboard /index.html.erb</p>` lines with the following:

```
<h1>Contests</h1>
<table class="table table-striped">
  <thead>
    <tr>
      <th>Name</th>
      <th>Criteria</th>
      <th>Winner</th>
      <th>Date</th>
    </tr>
```

```
        </thead>
        <tbody>
            <tr>
              <td>Customer Appreciation Giveaway</td>
              <td>Purchase made within last 30 days</td>
              <td>Order #1010, John Doe</td>
              <td>October 22, 2013</td>
            </tr>
        </tbody>
</table>
```

If we reload the dashboard page on our browser, we can see that our static HTML fits right in. Based on the form and table, we have an idea of the structure of the contest model we need to create, which consists of a few fields for storing the name, optional date range, optional product ID, optional max candidates, and the winning order ID. For the date of the contest, we'll just use the created_at column. Let's use the generator to create the model:

```
rails g model Contest name:string product_id:integer
start_date:datetime end_date:datetime max_results:integer
order_id:integer:index
```

3. Migrate the databases and annotate the model:

```
bundle exec rake db:migrate
```

```
bundle exec rake db:migrate RAILS_ENV=test
```

4. Update /app/models/contest.rb to make it relate to the orders, validate the presence of required fields, and also return contest criteria in a user friendly manner:

```
class Contest < ActiveRecord::Base
    belongs_to :order
    validates_presence_of :name

  def criteria
    results = []
    results << "Product Name: #{product_name}" if
    product_name.present?
    results << "Start Date: #{I18n.l start_date.to_date,
    format: :short}" if start_date.present?
    results << "End Date: #{I18n.l end_date.to_date,
    format: :short}" if end_date.present?
    results << "Max #: #{max_results}" if
    max_results.present?
    return results.join(', ')

  end
end
```

The `criteria` method uses conditional logic to create a string that summarizes the contest criteria. An example result would be `Product Name: Test Product, Max #: 50`.

5. Next, we'll need to add a method called `candidate_list` to create an array of valid candidates that we can send to the `ContestResults` class. Based on our form mockup, we need to be able to accept a product ID (or no product ID, which will translate into any product) and an optional date range. The tests for this method are found at `ch03_order_spec.rb` and the necessary factory code is at `ch03_order_factory.rb`, `ch03_order_item_factory.rb`, and `ch03_product_factory.rb`.

   Add the following code to `/app/models/order.rb`:

```ruby
# This method constructs the query based on
# the passed-in parameters
def self.candidate_list(params={})

  params[:order] ||= "order_date asc"
  orders = order(params[:order]).includes(:order_items)

  if params[:limit].present?
    orders = orders.limit(params[:limit].to_i)
  end

  if params[:product_id].present?
    orders = orders.where("order_items.shopify_product_id" =>
    params[:product_id].to_i)
  end

  if params[:start_date].present?
    orders = orders.where(["orders.order_date >= ?",
    params[:start_date]])
  end

  if params[:end_date].present?
    orders = orders.where(["orders.order_date <= ?",
    params[:end_date]])
  end

  # .pluck returns an array containing the specified field
  return orders.pluck(:id).uniq

end
```

This method builds the query based on the different options passed in via the `params` hash, and then returns an array of order IDs that qualify. The array can then easily be fed into our results method to choose a winner.

Due to the way the **ActiveRecord Query Interface** works, we're able to add conditions as needed based on the parameters, and nothing is executed against the database until we are ready.

You probably noticed that the parameters use the same names as the columns for a contest record even though it's on the order model. This is intentional to allow us to easily reconstruct a previous contest and pick a new winner.

6. Now that we have the model method completed, we can update the `DashboardController` to load the results and instantiate a new contest object for our form:

```
def index
  # Load past results in reverse order
  @contests = Contest.order("created_at desc")

  # Instantiate a new Contest so the form loads properly
  @contest = Contest.new
end
```

7. We also need to create a controller action and a corresponding route for the form to post to upon submission. As usual, we'll add the routing and controller tests first, and then create the corresponding action:

```
# This method creates a Contest and returns
# the winner(s) in the notice message
  def create_contest
    @contest = Contest.new(contest_params)
# Store the name of the product for easier readability
    @contest.product_name = Product.find_by_shopify_product_
    id(contest_params[:product_id]).try(:name) if contest_
    params[:product_id].present?
    respond_to do |format|
      if @contest.save
        # Pick a winner
        candidates = Order.candidate_list(params)
        contest_results = ContestResults.new(candidates)

        # Save the winner
        @contest.update_attribute(:order_id,
        contest_results.results)


        format.html { redirect_to root_path, notice: "Contest
        Winner: <a href='#{order_path(@contest.order)}'>#{@
```

```
    contest.order.email}</a>" }
    format.json { render action: 'show', status: :created,
    location: @contest }

  else
    format.html { redirect_to root_path, alert: "Unable to
    create a Contest" }
    format.json { render json: @contest.errors, status
    : :unprocessable_entity }
  end
end

end

private

def contest_params
  params.require(:contest).permit(:name, :product_id, :start_
  date, :end_date, :max_results, :order_id)
end
```

We need to make sure to add the corresponding route to the `/config` `/routes.rb` file below `get "dashboard/index"`:

```
post "create_contest" => 'dashboard#create_contest'
```

8. Finally, we need to update the UI to dynamically render the table and update the form markup to use Rails helpers for the form tag, labels, and input elements. The controller action will redirect to the dashboard page and place the results on the notice bar. Copy the code from `ch03_dashboard_index.html.erb` to `/app/views/dashboard/index.html.erb`.

You might have noticed that the `select` element didn't use the built-in Rails helper. In our case, we needed to use a default option, option groups, and a dynamic list. Rolling it manually was the simplest way to create this element inline, and also illustrates how Rails constructs the `id` and `name` attributes on input elements.

We can now check in our work and merge it with the `master` branch using the following commands:

```
git add --all
git commit -am "Contest Functionality"
git checkout master
git merge ch03_08_contests
git push
```

That was the last requirement! We can now import products and orders and run contests to pick winners based on a few different options. Let's deploy to Heroku so we can try things out in a production environment:

```
git push heroku master
heroku run rake db:migrate
```

Summary

In this chapter, we signed up for Shopify, talked about our development process, and knocked out several requirements for the application. This involved installing several gems, writing a test suite, and using the built-in Rails generators to jump-start our development.

We then created topic branches for each requirement and worked until we were satisfied that the requirement was met. After we built the pieces to connect to Shopify and import orders and products, we cleaned up the UI.

Finally, we implemented our contest logic, which we approached from the top down by creating a mockup of the form and results table. This allowed us to see exactly what was required to execute a contest, which made it possible to develop this feature quickly without building unnecessary functionality. We now have a working application that we can use to organize contests for a single store.

In the next chapter, we'll update the app to make it **multitenant** (supporting multiple stores), enable it to verify requests from Shopify and subscribe and respond to webhooks, and give our app a few other final touches before it goes live in the Shopify App Store.

4

Going Public

In the previous chapter, we successfully turned our website into a functioning private application. In this chapter, we are going to update our code to make the app support **multitenancy**. This means that one instance of the app will be able to service multiple Shopify accounts simultaneously, instead of requiring each store to have its own copy of the app. An example of this is the difference between a site such as Facebook (multitenant) and a program such as Microsoft Word (single tenant). Everyone logs in to the same Facebook app, but each computer needs its own copy of Word. The multitenant model should be familiar to you as most websites you use operate in this manner.

To support multiple shops, we will need to acquire and store each shop's API password in a secure manner. Each password will be different, so we'll use them in place of the private ones that we generated earlier.

Fortunately for us, Shopify already has a process in place to securely acquire the API password and install our app into a Shopify store, so we'll be able to add this piece fairly easily. We'll then add security methods to verify the HTTP requests and webhooks using code found on the Shopify wiki. Finally, we're also going to add code to subscribe to and process webhooks from Shopify.

High-level requirements

As we did earlier, we are going to create a list of requirements that we'll turn into sprints. We'll then create topic branches for each sprint. Finally, we'll merge our code into the `master` branch once we're satisfied that we've met all the requirements and that all of the tests have passed. For this chapter, our requirements are as following:

- Support multiple accounts
- Authorize user access to data
- Verify requests from Shopify

- Install from the Shopify App Store
- Subscribe to and process Shopify Webhooks

Supporting multiple accounts

We'll need to update our `Account` model by adding a few more columns to store additional information from Shopify. We'll also remove the `shopify_shared_secret` and `shopify_api_key` columns and store the values in global variables. As can be inferred from the name, this secret will be used whenever we need to make an API request or verify an incoming request from Shopify.

As usual, we'll make a topic branch for our work with the following command:

```
git checkout -b ch04_01_account_rework
```

We'll then use a migration to update the database with the following command:

```
rails g migration AccountRework
```

This generator will create a ruby file that we can use to add and remove columns from the `accounts` table. Copy and paste the following code into the migration file that was created by the preceding command:

```ruby
class AccountRework < ActiveRecord::Migration
  def change

    # These columns are not unique but global
    remove_column :accounts, :shopify_shared_secret
    remove_column :accounts, :shopify_api_key

    # We need to store more information about the shop
    add_column :accounts, :shopify_shop_id, :integer
    add_column :accounts, :shopify_shop_name, :string
    add_column :accounts, :shop_owner, :string
    add_column :accounts, :email, :string

    # Index commonly searched for fields
    add_index :accounts, :shopify_account_url
    add_index :accounts, :email

  end
end
```

(handwritten margin notes):
ACCOUNTS
· SP-SHOP_ID
· SP_SHOP_NAME
· SHOP OWNER
· GMAIL
· SP_ACC_URL
· GMAIL

This migration will update the database and add a couple of indexes that will make searching more efficient. We can now run the migration and annotate the models via the following command lines:

```
bundle exec rake db:migrate
```

```
bundle exec rake db:migrate RAILS_ENV=test
```

As expected, because we dropped the columns before updating our tests, some of them will immediately fail. This is precisely why we write tests. Ideally, we would have updated the tests first, but I wanted to illustrate how a test suite can act as a safety net. Once all the tests have passed again, we can be assured that the app works the same as it did before. Then, we can update the tests to reflect the new columns that we added when we removed the `shopify_api_key` and `shopify_shared_secret` columns.

> While you might be tempted to fix failing tests and add more for the new columns at the same time, don't do it. Changing more than one thing at a time is a recipe for confusion. Of course, following proper TDD best practices means that this sort of situation theoretically shouldn't happen because the updates would have been anticipated. However, in practice, it's a common event, especially in existing applications where test coverage is inadequate.

Now, we need to rework our code to store the API password and shared secret in our global variables and update any references to the removed columns. We're also going to store the current URL of our app in the configuration file so that we can use it to create endpoints for webhooks when registering with Shopify. Add the following lines of code (with your test shop values) to `/config/environments/development.rb`:

```
SHOPIFY_API_KEY = "123456789abcdefghijk"
SHOPIFY_SHARED_SECRET = "zyxvutsrq987654321"
DOMAIN = "http://localhost:3000"
```

For testing purposes, we're going to use fake values and place the following code in `/config/environments/test.rb`:

```
SHOPIFY_API_KEY = "123abc"
SHOPIFY_SHARED_SECRET = "test-secret"
DOMAIN = "http://localhost:3000"
```

These will be picked up the next time the web server is started (or restarted if it's already running).

For security purposes, sensitive production information such as passwords should never be checked into source control. Instead, this information should be stored in configuration files or environment variables that only exist on the server and are loaded at application startup. We'll store the values as Heroku environment variables and load them in `/config/environments/production.rb` with the following code:

```
SHOPIFY_API_KEY = ENV["SHOPIFY_API_KEY"]
SHOPIFY_SHARED_SECRET = ENV["SHOPIFY_SHARED_SECRET"]
DOMAIN = ENV["DOMAIN"]
```

And then we'll use the following Heroku toolbelt command to update the production environment (substitute the real values from our Shopify test store's private app settings as well as our Heroku app's URL):

```
heroku config:set SHOPIFY_API_KEY=123456789abcdefghijk

heroku config:set SHOPIFY_SHARED_SECRET=zyxvutsrq987654321

heroku config:set DOMAIN=http://contestapp.herokuapp.com
```

Now, we can rework the code to remove any references to the old database columns and replace them with our global variables. If we search the project for occurrences of `shopify_api_key` and `shopify_shared_secret`, we will see the variables referenced in the `ShopifyIntegration` class, the `Account` model and related controller, view files, and tests.

The following is what the rework of the relevant methods in the `ShopifyIntegration` class looks like:

```
attr_accessor :url, :password

def initialize(params)
  # Ensure that all the parameters are passed in
  %w{url password}.each do |field|
    raise ArgumentError.new("params[:#{field}] is required") if
    params[field.to_sym].blank?

    # If present, then set as an instance variable
    instance_variable_set("@#{field}", params[field.to_sym])
  end
end

# Uses the provided credentials to connect to Shopify
def connect

  # Initialize the gem
  ShopifyAPI::Session.setup({
  api_key: SHOPIFY_API_KEY,
  secret: SHOPIFY_SHARED_SECRET})
```

```
# Instantiate the session
session = ShopifyAPI::Session.new(@url, @password)

# Activate the Session so that requests can be made
return ShopifyAPI::Base.activate_session(session)

end
```

As can be seen, all that we had to do was update the `initialize` method to only acquire the URL and password. We also updated the `connect` method to use our global variables when appropriate.

After we've finished the rest of the rework and verified that the tests have passed, we are going to jump back on the TDD train for the next feature and update our test suite before making changes to the code. Hopefully, we'll see how doing it the test-driven way makes development easier because it gives us concrete requirements to satisfy and a definition of "done".

Let's update `/spec/factories/accounts.rb` to reflect the new `Account` fields with the following code:

```
FactoryGirl.define do
  factory :account do
    # Use a sequence to ensure unique values
    sequence :shopify_account_url do |n|
      "test-#{n}.myshopify.com"
    end
    shopify_password "MyString"
    created_at {DateTime.now}
    updated_at {DateTime.now}
    # Use a large random number to ensure unique values
    shopify_shop_id {rand 9999999}
    sequence :shopify_shop_name do |n|
      "shop_#{n}"
    end
    shop_owner "Bugs Bunny"
    # Use a sequence to ensure unique values
    sequence :email do |n|
      "owner_#{n}@example.com"
    end
  end
end
```

Now that we're going to be creating accounts directly through Shopify, we can completely remove `AccountsController` and related views from the app since they are now redundant. We will preserve the code that tests the connection to the Shopify API for a particular `Account`, since we'll be moving this feature over to `DashboardController` and turning the **Test Connection** button into a link at the bottom of the sidebar on the dashboard page.

The updated dashboard files of interest are called `ch04_dashboard_controller.rb`, `ch04_dashboard_controller_spec.rb`, and `ch04_dashboard_routing_spec.rb`.

Once our dashboard routing and view tests have passed again (we can ignore any other failed tests for now), we're going to remove the following files (we can use `git rm` as well, though this is not necessary):

- `/app/controllers/accounts_controller.rb`
- `/app/views/accounts/*`
- `/spec/controllers/accounts_controller_spec.rb`
- `/spec/requests/accounts_spec.rb`
- `/spec/routing/accounts_routing_spec.rb`
- `/spec/views/accounts/*`

 The asterisk (*) means that all files in that respective folder.

Note that we're still keeping the factory and model tests because they are needed to verify that the `Account` model is behaving correctly. One final piece of cleanup is to remove the unnecessary navigation link in `/app/views/layouts/application.html.erb` as follows:

```erb
<div class="container-fluid nav-collapse">
  <ul class="nav">
    <li><%= link_to "Products", products_path %></li>
    <li><%= link_to "Orders", orders_path %></li>
  </ul>
</div>
```

Once we're happy that the `Account` model has been properly reworked and all the tests have passed, we can commit the code, merge it into the `master` branch, and push it to the remote repository using the following commands:

```
git add --all
```

```
git commit -am "Reworked the Account model and related areas to support
multitenancy"
```

```
git checkout master
```

```
git merge ch04_01_account_rework
```

```
git push
```

Authorizing user access to data

Currently, the application loads all the contests, orders, and products in the database. This was acceptable before because the app was only linked to a single Shopify account. Now, we need to limit the information returned to the current `Account` model only. This way, when a store owner logs in to the app, they will only see their own information and will be unable to view any information from other shops.

To do this, we need to perform the following steps:

1. Make a topic branch for our work with the help of the following command:

   ```
   git checkout -b ch04_02_account_scoping
   ```

2. Add an `account_id` field to the `Contest`, `Product`, and `Order` models. We will do this by creating a migration to update the database with the following command:

   ```
   rails g migration AccountScoping
   ```

   Our migration needs to add an `account_id` field to any models that we want to protect. We'll also add the following database indexes on these new columns to make the queries more efficient:

   ```
   class AccountScoping < ActiveRecord::Migration
     def change
       add_column :orders,   :account_id, :integer
       add_column :products, :account_id, :integer
       add_column :contests, :account_id, :integer

       add_index :orders,   :account_id
       add_index :products, :account_id
       add_index :contests, :account_id
     end
   end
   ```

3. Run the following migrations for the development and test databases:

```
bundle exec rake db:migrate

bundle exec rake db:migrate RAILS_ENV=test
```

4. Set up the relationship between each of the models so we can take advantage of the `ActiveRecord` query interface. We'll add the following line to the `Order`, `Product`, and `Contest` models (found in the `/app/models` folder):

```
belongs_to :account
```

5. Add the corresponding lines to the `Account` model:

```
has_many :orders, :dependent => :destroy
has_many :products, :dependent => :destroy
has_many :contests, :dependent => :destroy
```

One consequence of adding the `account_id` field is that any existing records are now **orphaned**, which means they are not associated with an `Account` model, and will not show up in any of the scoped queries that we're about to implement. Just for kicks, we're going to fix the existing data using the Rails console rather than deleting the orphaned records.

6. Start up a Rails console session in a new terminal window with the following command:

```
rails console
```

7. Enter the following commands to fill the `account_id` field with the ID of the first account in the database:

```
account = Account.first

Order.update_all(["account_id = ?", account.id])

Product.update_all(["account_id = ?", account.id])

Contest.update_all(["account_id = ?", account.id])
```

8. Locate the places in our code where we are creating orders, products, and contests and add the correct account ID in the `account_id` field. We'll need to update our import methods in the `ShopifyIntegration` class.

Let's rework this service class to require `account_id`. First, we'll update our tests to reflect this new requirement, which you can see in `ch04_shopify_integration_spec.rb`. Then, we'll make the subsequent updates to the class itself, until our tests have all passed. The updated class can be found in `ch04_shopify_integration.rb`.

9. We're going to add a few methods to `ApplicationController` and expose some as helper methods that can also be used in our view files. The complete class is as shown:

```ruby
class ApplicationController < ActionController::Base
  # Prevent CSRF attacks by raising an exception.
  # For APIs, you may want to use :null_session instead.
  protect_from_forgery with: :exception

  helper_method :current_account, :logged_in?
  before_action :require_login

  ### Filters ###

  # This method is called before each controller action is
  # executed in order to ensure that the user is logged in
  def require_login
    redirect_to sessions_new_path unless current_account.present?
  end

  def login(account_id)
    session[:current_account_id] = account_id
  end

  def logged_in?
    current_account.present?
  end

  # Finds the Account with the ID stored in the session with the
  # key :current_account_id. This is a common way to handle user
  # login in a Rails application; logging in sets the session
  # value and logging out removes it.
  def current_account
    @_current_account ||= session[:current_account_id] &&
      Account.find_by(id: session[:current_account_id])
  end
end
```

10. For the controller rework, we need to change any class-level `ActiveRecord` queries to use the `current_account` helper that we created earlier. In /app/ controllers/products_controller.rb, we need to change the following methods to use the `current_account` scope:

```ruby
def index
  @products = current_account.products.all
```

```
  end

  def new
    @product = current_account.products.new
  end

  def create
    @product = current_account.products.new(product_params)
    [...]
  end

  def import
    # Connect to Shopify
    shopify_integration = ShopifyIntegration.new(
  url: current_account.shopify_account_url,
      password: current_account.shopify_password,
      account_id: current_account.id)
    [...]
  end

  def set_product
    @product = current_account.products.find(params[:id])
  end
```

We'll need to make similar updates to the order controller, which can be seen in ch04_orders_controller.rb. A high-level way to test that the scoping is working is to populate the database with a few records that have different values for account_id. Then, we'll make a request to the index action and ensure that only the records with current_account.id are returned. For example, the following is the OrdersController test for the index action (the full set of tests can be found in ch04_orders_controller_spec.rb. Keep in mind that some of these will fail until we complete the next step):

```
describe "GET index" do
    it "assigns scoped orders as @orders" do
      # Create an Account that will be loaded as the default
      account = FactoryGirl.create(:account)

      # Create 2 orders for the current account
      order1 = FactoryGirl.create(:order, account_id: account.id)
      order2 = FactoryGirl.create(:order, account_id: account.id)

      # And one for a different account
      order3 = FactoryGirl.create(:order, account_id: 100)

      get :index, {}, valid_session
      assigns(:orders).should eq([order1, order2])
    end
  end
```

As you can see, the previous code creates three orders, with two belonging to the same `Account` model. It then gets the `index` action and ensures that the `@orders` variable only consists of the two orders that belong to the currently logged in account.

In the final step, we'll create a way for our users to log in to their accounts. Rather than storing our own set of user login information we're going to allow logins directly from Shopify. This way, our storeowners won't have to remember another login and password, and any of their staff users in Shopify will be able to log in to our app with a single click. By default, the URL that our storeowners are redirected to for logging in to the app will be the same one that was used to install the app. All we have to do for now is remember to support a login to an existing account in our `install` method, and we're done with this part.

To keep things consistent, we're going to create a controller to handle the login and logout and display an error message if attempts are made to access pages in the app without being logged in. We'll then add a **filter** to our `ApplicationController` to ensure that the user is logged in before they can view any of the pages. A filter is a method that we want executed before or after a specific event.

Run the following command in the console window to create the controller:

```
rails generate controller Sessions new create destroy
```

As can be seen, we specified the three methods (`new`, `create`, and `destroy`) that we want the controller to have. Using the generator in this manner is a handy way to ensure that all the files we care about (views, tests, and routes) have been properly created as well. However, we need to make a tweak to the `/config/routes.rb` file to change the line that says `get "sessions/create"` to `post "sessions/create"`.

> Note that the convention is to keep the controller's action names limited to the following: `index`, `show`, `new`, `create`, `edit`, `update`, and `destroy`. This ensures that the code is easily understood by other developers because it keeps to best practices.

In place of the typical login screen, we're going to render a simple page with a form that initiates the authorize/install process in Shopify. This way, storeowners with existing accounts will be logged in automatically, and storeowners that do not have an account with us will have the opportunity to install the app. This form will also allow us to easily test our app as well as initiate installations from the app directly rather than relying on storeowners finding us in the App store.

Due to a limitation in Shopify that does not allow us to send messages to our development machine (at least, not without using dynamic DNS to map a domain to our local IP), we're going to add a small form to the login page that is only visible in development mode. This form will allow us to select the account that we want to impersonate.

The complete code can be copied from `ch04_sessions_new_01.html.erb` and the corresponding controller code in `ch04_sessions_controller.rb`. This sort of **backdoor** is a common way to shortcut complicated procedures in order to access a certain part of the app during development. Backdoors can often lead to unintended security vulnerabilities and should be used with extreme caution, and removed from the `production` code branch if possible.

It doesn't make sense to show the navigation for orders and products if the user is not logged in. Fortunately, we can easily hide this by checking for `current_account`. Remember the `logged_in?` method that we added to the `ApplicationController` earlier? We can use this helper to check for a logged-in account and if not found hide the navigation.

The following is the updated HTML code for the `navbar` element in `/app/view/layouts/application.html.erb`:

```
<div class="navbar navbar-fluid-top">
    <div class="navbar-inner">
```

```
<div class="container-fluid">
  <% if logged_in? %>
  <a class="btn btn-navbar" data-target=".nav-collapse"
  data-toggle="collapse">
    <span class="icon-bar"></span>
    <span class="icon-bar"></span>
    <span class="icon-bar"></span>
  </a>
  <% end %>
  <a class="brand" href="/">Contest App</a>
  <% if logged_in? %>
    <div class="container-fluid nav-collapse">
      <ul class="nav">
        <li><%= link_to "Products", products_path %></li>
        <li><%= link_to "Orders", orders_path %></li>
        <li><%= link_to "Logout", sessions_destroy_path %>
        </li>
      </ul>
    </div><!--/.nav-collapse -->
  <% end %>
</div>
  </div>
</div>
```

As can be seen, we're using the `logged_in?` helper method to hide both the collapsed menu as well as the regular navigation icon. Once we're satisfied that everything is working properly and all the tests have passed, we can commit the code, merge it into the master branch, and push it to the remote repository using the following commands:

```
git add --all
git commit -am "Added Account Scoping and login."
git checkout master
git merge ch04_02_account_scoping
git push
```

Verifying Shopify requests

Now that we will be handling installation requests from Shopify and subscribing to webhooks, it's a good idea to verify that the requests originate from Shopify and haven't been tampered with. There are two different types of requests that we need to authenticate:

- HTTP GET/POST requests (for example, an app installation request)
- Webhooks (for example, a new order was placed)

Normally, we might have added this code inline as part of the next two sprints, but I wanted to handle it separately in order to highlight the importance of security. Also, these methods are reusable for future apps as well, and developing the code with this encapsulation in mind will be beneficial.

Let's create a topic branch for our work with the following command:

```
git checkout -b ch04_03_shopify_verification
```

Verifying HTTP GET/POST requests

Shopify provides the Ruby code necessary to verify the first type of request. The code extracts a few elements from the `params` hash into an array, sorts them alphabetically, converts the array to a string, and then encrypts the string using our shared secret. This value is compared to the field that was passed with the request. If the values match, we can be assured that the request is valid.

We'll add the following tests to `/spec/services/shopify_integration_spec.rb` to handle HTTP requests. These tests will use hardcoded values that match the ones in `/config/environments/test.rb`. It's worth remembering that if any values in this file change, the tests will fail as a result, and you'll need to manually recalculate the correct hash to fix the specification. Refer to the following code:

```ruby
context "self.verify" do

  it "should return true if the signature matches" do
    # Assume we have the query parameters in a hash
    query_parameters = {
      shop: "some-shop.myshopify.com",
      code: "a94a110d86d2452eb3e2af4cfb8a3828",
      timestamp: "1337178173",
      signature: "929b77106a419bde96b151b318557a11"}

    ShopifyIntegration.verify(query_parameters).should be_true

  end

  it "should return false if the signature DOES NOT match" do
    # Assume we have the query parameters in a hash
    query_parameters = {
      shop: "some-shop.myshopify.com",
      code:  "a94a110d86d2452eb3e2af4cfb8a3828",
      timestamp: "1337178173",
      signature: "929b77106a419bde96b151b318557234"} # Changed

    ShopifyIntegration.verify(query_parameters).should be_false
  end

end
```

A simplified version (for clarity) of the code that Shopify provides is listed as follows:

```
def self.verify(params)
      hash = params.slice(:code, :shop, :signature, :timestamp)
      received_signature = hash.delete(:signature)
      # Collect the URL parameters into an array of elements
      calc = hash.collect { |k, v| "#{k}=#{v}" }
      # Sort the key/value pairs in the array
      calc = calc.sort
      # Join the array elements into a string
      calc = calc.join
      # Final calculated signature to compare against
      calc = Digest::MD5.hexdigest(SHOPIFY_SHARED_SECRET + calc)
      return calc == received_signature
end
```

This code will exist as a `class` method in our `/app/services/shopify_integration.rb` class. A `class` method is one that does not require an instance of the class in order to be invoked. Instead, we can simply call it using `ShopifyIntegration.verify(params)` from the controller action that received the request in order to decide whether or not to proceed.

Verifying webhook requests

The second type of verification we'll need to implement is for webhook requests. Though the topics vary, the method of verification is the same for all of them. The process is very similar to what we just did, in that we'll be receiving an encrypted hash from Shopify that we'll use to verify the contents of the request after we have performed some encryption ourselves. Fortunately, in this case, we don't need to reorder the parameters; instead, we can just take the entire body of the request and use the **SHA256** algorithm to generate a string that can be used for comparison. Again, Shopify provides this code on their wiki, but we're going to make a few tweaks to improve testability and abstraction.

We're going to create a `WebhookService` class in a new file at `/app/services/webhook_service.rb` by copying the code from `ch04_webhook_service`.
The following verification code from the Shopify wiki is listed below for review:

```ruby
def verify_webhook
  # TODO: disable this after launch
  return true if @request.headers['HTTP_X_SHOPIFY_TEST'].to_s ==
"true"

  # Make sure the encrypted header was passed in
  hmac_header = @request.headers['HTTP_X_SHOPIFY_HMAC_SHA256']
  return false if hmac_header.blank?

  # In order to verify the authenticity of the request
  # We need to compare the header hmac to one
  # We compute on the fly
  data = @request.body.read.to_s

  # Calculate the hmac using our shared secret and the body
  digest = OpenSSL::Digest::Digest.new('sha256')
  calculated_hmac = Base64.encode64(OpenSSL::HMAC.digest(
                            digest,
                            SHOPIFY_SHARED_SECRET,
                            data)).strip

  unless calculated_hmac == hmac_header
    return false
  end

  # Rewind the request body so that Rails can reprocess it
  @request.body.rewind
  return true
end
```

Before computing the hash, notice that the method checks for a header value that indicates that the request is not a test as well as ensuring that a hashed value has been passed in. If these two criteria are met, then the hash is computed using our shared secret and compared to the header value.

Finally, we need to rewind the request stream so that Rails can finish processing it. This is an important step because if we don't rewind it, the request stream will be at the end and no further data will be available.

Use the following commands to complete the sprint and deploy to production:

```
git add --all
git commit -am "Added Verification for HTTP and Webhook requests"
git checkout master
git merge ch04_03_shopify_verification
git push
git push heroku master
heroku run rake db:migrate
```

Installing from the Shopify App Store

Rather than requiring Shopify merchants to copy and paste their API credentials into our app's **Settings** page. Shopify has a handy and secure way for us to request access to a particular store, get the storeowner's permission, and programmatically receive the API credentials. The workflow is listed as follows:

1. The storeowner clicks on the **Install** button in the Shopify App Store.

2. Shopify redirects them to a special URL in our app, which then redirects back to Shopify with the API key of our app and a list of permissions we wish to have (for example, the ability to read order information and update products).

3. The storeowner is presented with a page in their Shopify admin that shows the access permissions that we've requested and allows them to approve it.

4. Once access is granted, Shopify posts back to our app with the shop address, a timestamp, and a temporary token. We use this token along with our shared secret to posts back to Shopify to complete the verification process.

5. Now that they've verified our identity with Shopify, the permanent API key for the shop is sent back in the response. We then use this key to make subsequent API calls in combination with our shared secret.

6. We'll do this right away to pull in a few pieces of data from the shop and store it locally.

Fortunately for us, there are code examples on the Shopify wiki that we can use as the starting point for these tasks. Let's create a topic branch with the following command and get to work:

```
git checkout -b ch04_04_shopify_installation
```

We need to create an App via our Shopify Partner account before proceeding. Once we log into the Partners area, we need to go to the Apps page and click on the **Create App** button. Fill out the form and be sure to set the Application Callback URL to `http://localhost:3000/shopify/install`. Then we'll update our configuration in `/config/environments/development.rb` as well as updating the Heroku environment variables with the new values for api key and shared secret.

We'll need to create a new controller to facilitate the Shopify installation process. For now, we'll only need two methods: `authorize` and `install`. To spice things up, we'll add the routes ourselves and create the controller file and tests from scratch rather than using the generator. The tests can be found in `ch04_shopify_controller_spec.rb` and `ch04_shopify_routing_spec.rb`. Add the following code to `/app/config/routes.rb`:

```
# Shopify routes
get 'shopify/authorize' => 'shopify#authorize'
post 'shopify/authorize' => 'shopify#authorize'
get 'shopify/install' => 'shopify#install'
post 'shopify/install' => 'shopify#install'
```

We'll support both GET and POST so that we can call the actions from either a link or a form post. Let's create the class in `/apps/controllers/shopify_controller.rb` as follows and add the `authorize` action:

```
class ShopifyController < ApplicationController

  # Skip the login requirement
  skip_before_filter :require_login
  skip_before_filter :verify_authenticity_token
  def authorize
    unless params[:shop].present?
      render :text => "shop parameter required" and return
    end
    # Redirect to the authorization page
    redirect_to "https://
    #{params[:shop].gsub(".myshopify.com","")}.myshopify.com
    admin/oauth/authorize?client_id=#{SHOPIFY_API_KEY}&
    scope=read_products,read_orders,read_customers"
  end
end
```

All we're doing is redirecting to a specific URL in Shopify and appending our API key as well as a list of the permissions we want. In this case, we just need to read `Customers`, `Orders`, and `Products`.

The `install` method that we need to write is a bit more complex. This method will complete the handshake with Shopify in order to receive the API password that we need to access the store's information. The process involves exchanging a few tokens as a means of verification. Again, we'll use the following sample code from the Shopify wiki to get us started:

```
def install

  # Initialize the connection to Shopify
  http = Net::HTTP.new(params[:shop], 443)
  http.use_ssl = true
  path = '/admin/oauth/access_token'

  # Include the relevant pieces of information
  data = {
    'client_id' => SHOPIFY_API_KEY,
    'client_secret' => SHOPIFY_SHARED_SECRET,
    'code' => params[:code]
  }

  # POST to Shopify in order to receive the permanent token
  response = http.post(path, data.to_query, headers)
  result = ActiveSupport::JSON.decode(response.body)

  # See if the Account already exists
  account = Account.find_by_shopify_account_url(params[:shop])

  # Update the existing Account if so
  if account.present?
    account.update_attributes(
    shopify_password: result["access_token"])
    else # Create a new account
    account = Account.create(
    shopify_shop_name: params[:shop],
    shopify_password: result["access_token"],
    shopify_account_url: params[:shop]
    )

  end

  # Reload to ensure we get the proper value for ID
  account.reload

  # Set this account as the active one
  login(account.id)
```

```
# Redirect to the dashboard
redirect_to dashboard_index_path

end
```

Update `/app/views/sessions/new.html.erb` with the code from
`ch04_sessions_new_02.html.erb`. Then reload the dashboard page
and type in the address of your Shopify test site in the form to authorize access.

Once the request is sent back to Shopify, the user will see something similar to the
following screenshot:

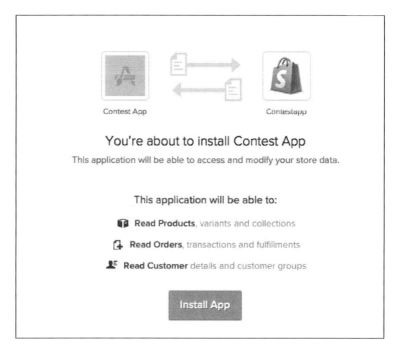

The permissions we asked for are listed, and the storeowner has an easy way to
grant access. Once we have access to the API, we can use it to pull information into
the new `Account` columns that we added earlier. We'll add the following method
to `/app/services/shopify_integration.rb` to accomplish the mapping to the
new `Account` structure:

```
def update_account
    shop = ShopifyAPI::Shop.current

    # Map the shop fields to our local model
    # Choosing clarity over cleverness
```

```
     account = Account.find @account_id

     account.shopify_shop_id = shop.id
     account.shopify_shop_name = shop.name
     account.shop_owner = shop.shop_owner
     account.email = shop.email

     account.save
  end
```

The updated tests can be found in `ch04_shopify_integration_spec.rb`. Let's update our `install` controller action to call this method after we've been granted access to the API. We'll add the following lines before `redirect_to dashboard_index_path`:

```
# Use our new credentials to grab account information
shopify_service = ShopifyIntegration.new(
                url: account.shopify_account_url,
                password: account.shopify_password,
                account_id: account.id)
shopify_service.connect
shopify_service.update_account
```

According to our tests, we can now respond to an authorized request initiated by a storeowner, request appropriate permissions from Shopify, and complete the verification process. In reality, Shopify doesn't allow us to use our development environment as the endpoint for the `authorize` and `install` URLs, which is why we had to use `FakeWeb` to simulate the responses. In order to test this out in the real world, we'll need to deploy to Heroku and update our app listing in Shopify to point to our production site.

To update our listing, we can head over to our Shopify partner account, go to our app, and click on the **Edit App Settings** button. We can now update the `Application Callback` URL to point to the Heroku URL as shown in the following screenshot:

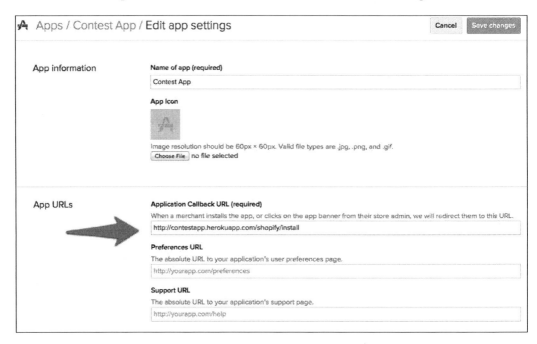

Once this is done, we'll be able to do an end-to-end test of the installation process using the form we added earlier.

Let's commit our work and test it out in production using the following commands:

```
git add --all
git commit -am "Completed the Shopify authorization and
installation process."
git checkout master
git merge ch04_04_shopify_installation
git push
```

We can deploy to Heroku and run any migrations by executing the following two commands:

```
git push heroku master
heroku run rake db:migrate
```

Subscribing to and processing Shopify Webhooks

In addition to responding to installation requests, we also need to subscribe and respond to webhooks sent from Shopify. For example, when a storeowner uninstalls our app from their store, we want to receive a **JSON** notification from Shopify that we can use to remove their account from our database.

> A more user-friendly option would be to send out an e-mail with a link to confirm the removal of their account. This way, if the uninstall was accidental, everything isn't purged immediately. Given the scope of this book, however, we're going to keep it simple and leave that as homework.

We'll be able to use the API code we already have in place in the `ShopifyIntegration` class to add the creation of webhook subscriptions. As usual, let's start off by creating a topic branch with the following command:

```
git checkout -b ch04_05_shopify_webhooks
```

To create a webhook, all we need to do is provide a URL where we'll receive the webhooks as well as the topic that we want to subscribe to. In our case, this is `app/uninstalled`. The endpoint will require a new controller as well as new routes. You can copy the code from `ch04_webhooks_controller_spec.rb`, `ch04_webhooks_controller.rb`, `ch04_webhooks_routing_spec.rb`, and `ch04_routes.rb`.

You may recall that we created a global constant called `DOMAIN` that stores the address of our website. We can use this to create the URL endpoint where we want the webhooks to be sent. The method we need to add to `/apps/services/shopify_integration.rb` is listed as follows:

```
def setup_webhooks

  webhook_url = "#{DOMAIN}/webhooks/uninstall"

  begin

    # Remove any existing webhooks
    webhooks = ShopifyAPI::Webhook.find :all
    webhooks.each do |webhook|
      webhook.destroy if webhook.address.include?(DOMAIN)
    end
```

```
        # Set up our webhooks
        ShopifyAPI::Webhook.create(
        address: webhook_url,
        topic: "app/uninstalled",
        format: "json"
        )

    rescue => ex
        puts "--------------"
        puts ex.message
    end
end
```

Now, whenever a storeowner uninstalls our app, we will receive a JSON notice to the WebhooksController#uninstall method. This method will process the webhook and use a new method called process_uninstall in our WebhookService class to call the destroy method on the specified Account. While we could have called the destroy method from within the WebhooksController, we're going to go ahead and use a service class to lay the foundation for processing more types of webhooks in the future. We also need to remember to call setup_webhooks in our ShopifyController.

Copy the code from ch04_webhook_service.rb, ch04_webhook_service_spec.rb, and ch04_shopify_controller.rb to the matching files in our project.

Let's wrap up the last sprint and deploy to production as follows:

```
git add --all
git commit -am "Completed the Shopify Webhook integration"
git checkout master
git merge ch04_05_shopify_webhooks
git push
git push heroku master
```

Summary

In this chapter, we reworked our app to support multitenancy, which means that multiple Shopify stores can use it simultaneously with their data kept private from other storeowners. This involved the adding of additional fields to the Account model and the scoping of database queries to only return results associated with the currently logged-in account. We also changed the way we gain access to the Shopify API, added verification steps to ensure that our app is secure, and removed redundant pages.

We created an easy way for people to install the app to their store as well as log in with a single click.

We're just about ready to publish the app and let people use it with their live shops. In the final chapter of the book, we'll complete the remaining steps necessary to monetize the app and create a listing in the Shopify App Store.

5

App Billing and Publication

We covered a lot of ground in the last two chapters. Our vanilla Rails application went through several sprints and grew to be a multitenant, API-consuming, contest-creating beast!

In this chapter, we'll complete the final steps towards the first public release of the application. We will be adding free and paid plans and setting up billing via the Shopify API.

At this point a private **beta** might be in order, where a few shops are invited to try the app for free and provide feedback before we make it available to all Shopify users. A beta release is a great way to create awareness of the application and get people excited about its official release. However, equally valuable (or more so) is the helpful feedback from users that understand that the app may have bugs/rough edges rather than complaints from users expecting a polished and production-ready experience.

 Users are more than happy to be included in the creation/refinement of a service that they plan on using, especially if the only cost to them is their time.

With or without a beta, the final step is to publish the app in the Shopify App Store (`http://apps.shopify.com`) so that any shop owner can try it out. To do this, we'll need to create graphics, screenshots, and marketing copy. We'll also fill out details about price and support contacts to give prospective customers the full picture.

High-level requirements

We're going to continue to work in topic branches, write tests, and verify our features before merging them into the `master` branch for deployment. In this chapter, we're going to complete the following requirements:

- Add free and paid plans
- Integrate with the Shopify Billing API
- Publish our listing in the Shopify App Store

Adding free and paid plans

We're going to offer two options to our users: a free plan that allows the creation of three `Contests` per month and a paid plan that allows the creation of unlimited `Contests`. In practice, our application might have multiple plans that offer different levels or features to encourage users to upgrade as their business grows, but for now, we'll keep it simple.

As usual, we'll need to create our topic branch as follows before making any code changes:

```
git checkout -b ch05_01_plan_options
```

Facilitating these two plans is simple. We need to add an attribute to the `Account` model to track whether or not it is a paid one. We will accomplish this by creating and executing a migration using the following commands:

```
rails g migration AddPlanToAccounts paid:boolean
bundle exec rake db:migrate
bundle exec rake db:migrate RAILS_ENV=test
```

Don't forget to update `/spec/factories/account_factory.rb` and `/spec/models/account_spec.rb` to reflect the addition of these fields.

In practice, the maximum number of allowed contests per month might be kept in a database table or configuration file so it could be updated later. However, we're going to store it in a **constant**, just like we do our Shopify credentials and domain name. Add the following line at the bottom of `/config/environment.rb` and then restart the Rails server to load it in:

```
MAX_CONTESTS_PER_MONTH = ENV["MAX_CONTESTS_PER_MONTH"] || 3
```

Next, we'll create a simple page where the user can pick the plan that they want. At this point, it may occur to you that we are recreating the account pages that we removed earlier. This is part of the iterative process; you may find that a piece of code removed in a previous sprint ends up being needed later. This is perfectly acceptable; it's better to keep the code base clean and targeted rather than have unused code around just in case. As you'll see, it's only a matter of issuing a few commands and making a few tweaks to recreate the code we need. If it ended up being more work than that, we could always look at the past commits in the source code where we removed the code related to the Account pages and copy it from there.

We're going to use the handy Rails generator to stub out the controller, tests, and views, and then we'll simply copy the relevant code from the existing Order code and modify it to suit our needs. We are once again going to use the built-in Rails generator by executing the follow command:

```
rails g controller Accounts edit update
```

Since we specified the controller actions that we wanted (edit and update), Rails already added the routes for us at /config/routes.rb. However, we need to adjust them before we can proceed. Consider the following two lines:

```
get "accounts/edit"
get "accounts/update"
```

Replace the preceding lines with the following:

```
get "account"=> 'accounts#edit'
patch "account"=> 'accounts#update'
put "account"=> 'accounts#update'
```

The code for the updated tests can be found in ch05_accounts_routing_spec.rb and ch05_accounts_controller_spec_v1.rb.

As before, we'll need to update the navigation in /apps/views/layouts/application.html.erb to allow access to these pages. Update the navigation unordered list to match the following:

```
<ul class="nav">
  <li><%= link_to "Products", products_path %></li>
  <li><%= link_to "Orders", orders_path %></li>
  <li><%= link_to "My Account", account_path %></li>
  <li><%= link_to "Logout", sessions_destroy_path %></li>
</ul>
```

We don't want the user to be able to inadvertently update their `Account` and change either `shopify_account_url` or `shopify_password`, which would break the connection to Shopify, but we still need them to be able to upgrade or downgrade as needed. To accomplish this, we're going to streamline the `update` form and modify the protected attributes to ensure that only the `paid` column can be updated. The code for the views and controller can be found in `ch05_accounts_form.html.erb` (which needs to be created as to `/app/views/accounts/_form.html.erb`), `ch05_accounts_edit.html.erb`, and `ch05_accounts_controller_v1.rb` (which corresponds to `/app/controllers/accounts_controller.rb`).

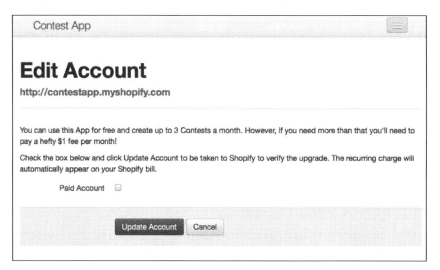

The next step is to create a way to limit the number of `Contests` that can be run per billing period. We will use a simple query that returns the number of `Contests` created within a specified date range to determine whether or not a user can create any more `Contests`.

The instance method for the query will be part of the `Account` model and looks like the following:

```
def contests_run(start_date, end_date)
return self.contests.where([
  "contests.created_at >= ? AND contests.created_at <= ?",
  start_date.beginning_of_day,
  end_date.end_of_day
  ]).count
end
```

The code builds the query by setting the boundaries for the `created_at` column based on the `start_date` and `end_date` variables. Then, it returns the count as an integer for easy comparison.

 By keeping the query generic, we'll be able to create reports later that reuse the same code, which means less work for us!

To enforce our rule, we're going to add checks at the `View` and `Controller` level. If an account has reached its limit for the current billing period, we're going to hide the create `Contest` form and show a message instead. We'll also add a check at the `Controller` level to provide feedback in the case where someone posted directly to our server in an attempt to illicitly create a contest.

This code is similar to what we used in the `production.rb` environment to load values from the Heroku ENV variables, except that it has an additional bit of logic to default to a value of 3 if the ENV variable isn't defined. We should encapsulate the logic that is used to check for the ability to create `Contests` so that the code is in one location. Let's add a method to the `Account` model as follows:

```
def can_create_contests?
    return true if self.paid?   # Paid Accounts have no limitations
    return (contests_run(DateTime.now - 1.month, DateTime.now) <
        MAX_CONTESTS_PER_MONTH)
end
```

This method checks to see if it's a paying account, and if not, ties together our generic query method and MAX_CONTESTS_PER_MONTH to determine whether or not the account is allowed to create any more contests. This logic could also reside in a helper method, concern class, or service class, depending on your preference. For the sake of simplicity, we'll put it in the model for now.

The updated controller code that uses this method as a security check before creating a contest can be found at `ch05_dashboard_controller.rb`. The updated view file can be found at `ch05_dashboard_index.html.erb` and along with the updated spec file in `ch05_account_spec.rb`.

Once all of our specs have passed and we're satisfied that we've completed this sprint, it's time to merge our branch back into `master` using the following commands:

```
git add --all
git commit -am "Added free and paid plans"
```

```
git checkout master
git merge ch05_01_plan_options
git push
```

Integrating with the Shopify Billing API

Shopify offers the ability to charge our customers as an add-on to their total Shopify bill. This allows app creators to easily earn money without having to set up a merchant account, deal with PCI compliance, or the myriad of other fun tasks associated with accepting funds online. However, this ease of use and reduced liability comes at a price: Shopify currently takes a 20 percent commission off of all charges created via the API.

Shopify allows us to create two different types of charges: one-time or recurring. One-time charges are used for things such as in-app purchases or upgrades. Recurring charges are meant for apps that offer monthly subscriptions, and Shopify is nice enough to handle proration for us in the case where a user upgrades in the middle of a billing period.

Before we dive in, let's go ahead and create our topic branch to store our work as follows:

```
git checkout -b ch05_02_billing_api
```

From the Shopify wiki (`http://docs.shopify.com/api/tutorials/shopify-billing-api#how-it-works`), we can see that the workflow consists of the following steps (consolidated for brevity):

1. We need to create a charge to be issued to the shop owner. Shopify will verify the charge and return a `confirmation_url`, which we will use to redirect the storeowners to a page where they can accept or decline the charge.

2. When a shop owner accepts or declines the charge, they will be sent to the `return_url`. The `return_url` contains an `id` for the charge that we'll use to activate it (assuming the shop owner accepted it) and capture our funds. Failure to activate the charge will result in the charge not appearing on the shop owner's invoice, and consequently, we will not get paid.

We're going to opt for a recurring charge of $1 a month to run unlimited contests. We'll need to expand our `ShopifyIntegration` class to include the creation of a `RecurringApplicationCharge` via the Shopify API. We'll need to store the charge's ID in our accounts table in order to be able to retrieve and verify the acceptance of the charge via the Shopify API.

To do this, we need to create and execute a migration with the following commands:

```
rails g migration AddChargeIdToAccounts charge_id:integer
```

```
bundle exec rake db:migrate

bundle exec rake db:migrate RAILS_ENV=test
```

In the next step, we need to add a method to `/app/services/shopify_integration.rb` to create the charge and return the confirmation URL from Shopify as follows:

```
def create_charge(amount, is_test)
  return_url = "#{DOMAIN}/shopify/confirm"

  # Create the charge
  charge = ShopifyAPI::RecurringApplicationCharge.create(
    name: "Contest App Paid Membership",
    price: amount.to_f,
    return_url: return_url,
    test: is_test ? true : nil
  )

  # Store the charge id for future reference
  account = Account.find @account_id
  account.update_attribute(:charge_id, charge.id)

  # Return the unique confirmation URL
  return charge.confirmation_url
end
```

This method creates a recurring charge, stores `charge_id` in the database for future reference, and returns `confirmation_url` as the result of the method invocation. We can easily integrate this into our `AccountsController#update` method to immediately redirect the user if they decide to upgrade, which we will do shortly.

 The is_test parameter exists because Shopify doesn't allow us to actually charge test shops with real transactions. So, for development purposes, we need to be able to pass in the test flag with our request.

We also need to add a method that removes the charge if the user downgrades to the free plan. Add the following method below the `create_charge` method in `/app/services/shopify_integration.rb`:

```
# This method destroys the recurring charge in Shopify
def delete_charge(charge_id)
  begin
    charge=ShopifyAPI::RecurringApplicationCharge.find (charge_id)
  rescue
  end
```

```
    # Ensure that the charge exists
    # trying to destroy it
    if charge.present?
      return charge.destroy
    else
      return true
    end
  end
```

The updated `ShopifyIntegration` class and related tests can be found in
`ch05_shopify_integration.rb` and `ch05_shopify_integration_spec.rb`.
Additionally, we need to modify the `AccountsController#update` method to
create the recurring charge when the user upgrades and to delete the charge if they
downgrade. The updated controller can be found in `ch05_accounts_controller_`
`v2.rb` (which corresponds to `/app/controllers/accounts_controller.rb`)
and the updated spec in `ch05_accounts_controller_spec_v2.rb`.

The following is a screenshot of what the shop owner will see when we redirect them
to confirm the charge. It looks ugly because we haven't uploaded an icon for our app,
which we'll do as part of filling out the listing in just a bit.

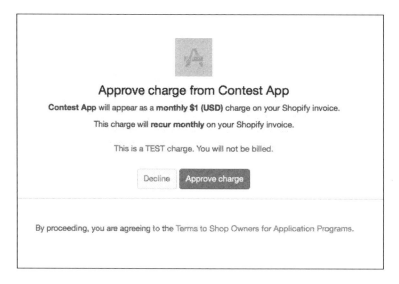

Next, we need to add a `confirm` action to our `ShopifyController` to receive the
postback from Shopify that contains the `charge_id` value so that we can verify
whether the merchant accepted it or not. If the charge was accepted, we need to
activate it via the Shopify API and then set the `paid` flag for the `Account` model. If
the merchant did not accept the charge, then we need to mark their account as unpaid.

Copy the routes from `ch05_routes.rb` to `/config/routes.rb`. The updated controller code can be viewed in `ch05_shopify_controller.rb` and the related tests in `ch05_shopify_controller_spec.rb`.

Supporting recurring charges

Once the recurring charge is under way, the following situations can occur:

- A recurring charge was declined because the shop owner didn't pay their Shopify bill

- A recurring charge was declined because they completely closed their Shopify account

- The shop owner downgraded from paid back to free in the middle of the billing cycle

These are business decisions that will drive the technical solution. Once you've decided how you want to handle these, you can build the test suite to simulate the different use cases before writing the code and making releases.

Once all of our tests pass and we're satisfied that we've completed this sprint, it's time to merge our code back into `master` as follows:

```
git add --all
git commit -am "Added support for Shopify Billing API"
git checkout master
git merge ch05_02_billing_api
git push
```

Publishing in the Shopify App Store

The final step is to fill out a listing for our app and submit it to the Shopify App Store. This listing includes the marketing copy, screenshots, icons, keywords, and pricing information. It's very important to make the listing as appealing as possible because this is the first impression most users will have of our app.

The images will need to conform to the size and resolution specifications listed on the form, so contact a graphical designer if this is beyond your skill set. Additionally, have someone read over the marketing copy to check for spelling and grammatical errors as well as coherence and readability. Remember that this listing will be the first impression you make to a majority of the Shopify storeowners.

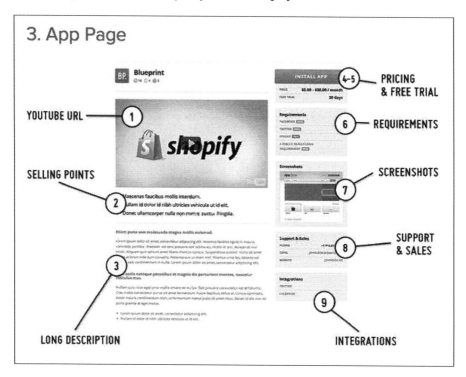

Once the listing is complete, all you need to do is submit it to Shopify and wait for it to be published. Once it's live, you'll want to do an end-to-end test to ensure that everything works as expected. Create a new shop via your Partner Account and go through the entire installation process from start to finish. Create a few test products and orders, and run a contest or two.

As you learned earlier, test shops can't be charged using the Billing API, so you'll need to either use a real one or start a trial for one of your test shops in order to make sure the charge shows up properly.

If you were able to do all of this without an issue, congratulations you made it!

Summary

This chapter marks the launch of Version 1.0 of our app!

We added a free and paid option and integrated with the Shopify Billing API for monetization. We wrapped up by spending some quality time creating a listing in the Shopify App Store that highlights the features of our app, entices storeowners to install it, and provides relevant information on pricing and support.

This book intentionally focused on the back-end programming related to creating an app and relied heavily on the Twitter Bootstrap generators to provide a basic UI. The upshot of using a popular library such as Bootstrap means that we'll be able to modify the CSS (or hire a designer) to improve the look and feel of the app fairly easily. Shopify maintains a list of experts, which is a great place to find a designer or developer to help you build your app. You can read reviews, compare rates, and see a portfolio of recent projects for each expert at `http://experts.shopify.com`.

Good luck!

Index

Thank you for buying
Shopify Application Development

About Packt Publishing

Packt, pronounced 'packed', published its first book "*Mastering phpMyAdmin for Effective MySQL Management*" in April 2004 and subsequently continued to specialize in publishing highly focused books on specific technologies and solutions.

Our books and publications share the experiences of your fellow IT professionals in adapting and customizing today's systems, applications, and frameworks. Our solution based books give you the knowledge and power to customize the software and technologies you're using to get the job done. Packt books are more specific and less general than the IT books you have seen in the past. Our unique business model allows us to bring you more focused information, giving you more of what you need to know, and less of what you don't.

Packt is a modern, yet unique publishing company, which focuses on producing quality, cutting-edge books for communities of developers, administrators, and newbies alike. For more information, please visit our website: www.packtpub.com.

About Packt Open Source

In 2010, Packt launched two new brands, Packt Open Source and Packt Enterprise, in order to continue its focus on specialization. This book is part of the Packt Open Source brand, home to books published on software built around Open Source licenses, and offering information to anybody from advanced developers to budding web designers. The Open Source brand also runs Packt's Open Source Royalty Scheme, by which Packt gives a royalty to each Open Source project about whose software a book is sold.

Writing for Packt

We welcome all inquiries from people who are interested in authoring. Book proposals should be sent to author@packtpub.com. If your book idea is still at an early stage and you would like to discuss it first before writing a formal book proposal, contact us; one of our commissioning editors will get in touch with you.

We're not just looking for published authors; if you have strong technical skills but no writing experience, our experienced editors can help you develop a writing career, or simply get some additional reward for your expertise.

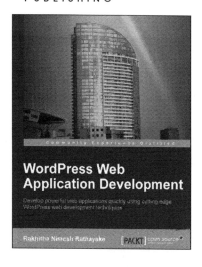

WordPress Web Application Development

ISBN: 978-1-78328-075-9   Paperback: 376 pages

Develop powerful web applications quickly using cutting-edge WordPress web development techniques

1. Develop powerful web applications rapidly with WordPress.

2. Practical scenario-based approach with ready-to-test source code.

3. Learning how to plan complex web applications from scratch.

Instant E-commerce with OpenCart: Build a Shop

ISBN: 978-1-78216-968-0   Paperback: 70 pages

A fast-paced, practical guide to setting up your own shop with OpenCart

1. Learn something new in an Instant! A short, fast, focused guide delivering immediate results.

2. Install and configure OpenCart correctly.

3. Tackle difficult tasks such as payment gateways, shipping options, product attributes, and managing orders.

Please check **www.PacktPub.com** for information on our titles

Magento Beginner's Guide
Second Edition

ISBN: 978-1-78216-270-4   Paperback: 320 pages

Learn how to create a fully featured, attractive online store with the most powerful open source solution for e-commerce

1. Install, configure, and manage your own e-commerce store.

2. Extend and customize your store to reflect your brand and personality.

3. Handle tax, shipping, and custom orders.

Instant E-Commerce with Magento: Build a Shop

ISBN: 978-1-78216-486-9   Paperback: 52 pages

A fast-paced, practical guide to building your own shop with Magento

1. Learn something new in an Instant! A short, fast, focused guide delivering immediate results.

2. Learn how to install and configure an online shop with Magento.

3. Tackle difficult tasks such as payment gateways, shipping options, and custom theming.

Please check **www.PacktPub.com** for information on our titles

Printed in Great Britain
by Amazon